Get Creative with

Cubase SX/SL

Composing and arranging with Cubase SX/SL

Keith Gemmell

PC Publishing

PC Publishing
Export House
130 Vale Road
Tonbridge
Kent TN9 1SP
UK

Tel 01732 770893
Fax 01732 770268
email info@pc-publishing.com
web site http://www.pc-publishing.com

First published 2003

© PC Publishing

ISBN 1 870775 864

British Library Cataloguing in Publication Data
A catalogue record for this book is available from the British Library

Cover design by Michelle Raki

Printed and bound in Great Britain by Biddles, Guildford

Preface

Welcome to *Get Creative with Cubase SX/SL*. Two questions:

1 Do you want to learn the basics of composition and arranging? The nuts and bolts as it were.
2 Do you also want to learn how to sequence, record and mix your compositions effectively within Cubase SX/SL?

If your answer to those questions is yes, this book will help you do both in a practical and enjoyable way. Nothing stuffy here!

There's an old proverb: *I hear and I forget, I see and I remember, I do and I understand.*

That's the essence of this book. Doing the projects and comparing your results along the way to the examples on the CD will provide you with a valuable insight into the creative process. What's more, you will be learning how to use Cubase SX/SL at the same time. Do and you will understand.

Two things are dealt with here:

1 The creative process, conceiving the ideas and developing them.
2 The production process, capturing, shaping and manipulating those ideas within Cubase SX/SL.

Both elements overlap and this book could just as easily have been entitled *Composing and Arranging with Cubase SX/SL*. There's no doubt that much of today's music is produced this way. The most obvious use is in the pop, techno and dance genres. However this is not the only use. Cubase SX/SL and similar music software production programs are used to record music for computer games, TV soundtracks, advertising jingles, radio drama and multimedia presentations, to name just a few. This book is aimed at helping musicians and students interested in writing for those kind of markets with the composition process; how to get the ideas in the first place and develop, record and mix them into a satisfying whole. Everything, the sequencing, the audio recording, the effects, dynamic processing and mixing, is done within Cubase SX/SL itself. Of course you do not have to actually do the projects if you don't want to. The text can be followed and a great deal learned by just loading and examining the example files.

Acknowledgments

Thanks to Risto Sampola of Steinberg UK, Arbiter Pro Audio (www.steinberguk.com), and Marcus Farny at Pocketfuel (www.pocketfuel.com).

Contents

How to use this book and CD

Equipment needed

All that's needed is a Mac or PC powerful enough to run a version of Cubase SX/SL equipped with a suitable sound card, a large, fast hard drive and decent monitor speakers. A keyboard and MIDI interface will be needed for working through the projects. Some of these include audio recording as an option. For this you will need a microphone and possibly an external mixer.

Most projects contain MIDI tracks, and for this you will need a General MIDI sound source. This can be a keyboard with on-board GM sounds, a sound card containing a GM sound set, a software synthesiser such as QuickTime Musical Instruments or an external sound module such as a Roland Sound Canvas.

The scheme of things

The book and accompanying CD are integral parts of Get Creative with Cubase SX/SL. Much of the time you will need to use both along with a copy of Cubase SX/SL running on your computer. This is most certainly the case with the sixteen chapters containing projects. Other chapters containing general reading matter also contain references to examples on the CD but make sense away from the computer.

If you already possess a working knowledge of Cubase SX/SL and MIDI sequencing then you may be tempted to skip the first few chapters and projects. That's OK but there is much to be gained, from a musical standpoint, by working through them.

Where possible, for clarity, all Cubase SX/SL functions are referred to using the program's menus. For example the instruction 'Use the VST Dynamic plug-in' would be followed by the menu command in square brackets: [Audio > Plug-ins > dynamics > VST Dynamics] (Figure 0.1). Power users can speed things up by using the many keyboard shortcuts and alternative methods available (see Appendix 2). There's usually more than one way of doing things in Cubase SX/SL.

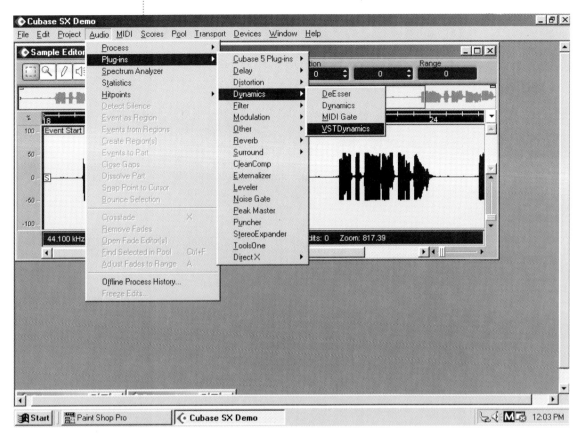

Figure 0.1 Opening the VST Dynamic plug-in.

The CD

The CD is compatible with both PC and Apple Mac computers and contains:

- Audio Files supplied in AIF – Audio Interchange File – format (with the extension .aif)
- Cubase SX/SL project files (with the extension .cpr)
- ReCycle files (with the extension .rex)
- Full demo version of Cubase SX (PC version)

The CD files are arranged in folders, relevant to the project or chapter to which they relate. Most chapters refer to musical examples contained on the CD. To examine them, copy the appropriate folder across to your computer desktop or some other location. It is particularly important that all the files contained in a folder are copied across and that they remain in their respective folders, particularly the audio files. Cubase SX/SL 'remembers' where they are situated and if they are moved, problems are likely to arise.

The Projects

The projects are a vital part of *Get Creative with Cubase SX/SL*. Each one builds on the techniques discussed in previous chapters and new Cubase SX/SL skills are progressively introduced.

- Projects 1 – 3 are concerned with MIDI sequencing skills. Three different styles of music are recorded – a rock band, a classical ensemble and a jazz funk band.
- Projects 4 – 9 are concerned with composition and arranging. In each one, a composition is built from scratch using a predetermined assignment. For example, the brief in project 5 instructs us to compose music for a soundtrack using minimalist techniques.
- Project 10 is concerned with the business of producing a readable score and parts from the Score Editor section of Cubase SX (not everything here is relevant to SL which has reduced score and notation features). A previous project, number 6, is used as a basis for the work.
- Projects 11 – 16 are solely concerned with the business of creative audio editing. These include such tasks as time stretching, pitch shifting and groove quantize.

All the projects follow a similar pattern and begin with a list of Musical Objectives and Cubase SX/SL skills. This is followed by a list of instructions headed Preparation. The first two instructions are always the same. In Project 5, for example:

- From the CD, copy the folder named 'project 5' to your desktop.
- Inside the 'project 5' folder you'll find a file named 'template5.cpr'. Open it and use it for this project.
- Create a folder in which to save your own files as you work through the project.

OK, here's the scenario. A computer game company has commissioned you to compose the music for a scene in their latest historical title set in Elizabethan times. The piece must run for a minimum of three minutes.

Each project contains a series of 'Takes'. These are usually an instruction to record something in Cubase SX/SL. At the beginning of each take is a list of settings for the Project window. For example Project 5, Take 1 looks like this.

Take 1

Track 1: (chn: 1) Guitar 1.
Quantize Selector: 1/8 Note.
Inspector: [out: GM] [chn: 1] [prg: 25] Nylon String Guitar.
Transport panel: (L) 1.01.01 (R) 5.01.01 Activate AQ.

The first line tells us which track to select, its instrument name and MIDI channel number (Figure 0.2). Next comes the Quantize Selector (on the Toolbar) with any quantize settings needed for the recording (Figure 0.3). This is followed by the Inspector settings. These usually contain the MIDI output – GM sound source or VST Instrument – MIDI channel, program number and name (Figure 0.4). Lastly, the Transport panel information, which is usually just the locator settings (Figure 0.5).

Figure 0.2 Track 1.

Figure 0.3 Quantize Selector

Figure 0.4 Inspector settings

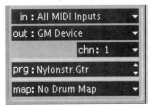

Figure 0.5 Locator settings

Figure 0.6 Preferences, MIDI Chase Events Filter

You then follow the text and perform the take itself. At the completion of a take there is always an instruction to save the work. In Project 5 it is:

- Save Project – compare with 5.1.cpr.

At this point you:

1 Save your work as a Cubase SX/SL Project file.
2 Compare it with the example Project file – in the project 5 folder copied over from the CD. It will not sound exactly the same as yours because you will have played it differently. However, it should be something similar. If you are happy with the result then close down the example Project File and continue with the project.

Each time a take is completed follow the same procedure and save your work as a Project file. The comparison Project file will always correspond to where you are in the project. If your version has gone astray in some way, you can always continue by working on the example instead.

Preferences

	MIDI-Chase Events Filter

Audio
  Broadcast Wave
  Time Stretch Tool
Editing
  Tool Modifiers
Event Display
  Audio
  MIDI
  Video
MIDI
  Function Parameters
  Chase Events Filter
  Filter
Scores
	Filter
	☑ Note
	☐ Poly Pressure
	☐ Controller
	☐ Program Change
	☐ Aftertouch
	☐ Pitchbend
	☑ Sysex

General MIDI

General MIDI has been used for the MIDI content in the projects and examples where conventional instrument sounds are required and the included VST Instruments are not suitable – acoustic piano for example.

When you load a project file example or template you will notice that the outputs for General MIDI are not connected (Figure 0.7). This leaves you free to use your own GM sound source. Please bear in mind that sound quality and volume levels vary from one GM sound source to another. You may have to adjust volume, chorus and reverb controls slightly for a pleasing balance.

Figure 0.7

The Universal Sound Module

If you don't have access to a General MIDI sound source you can use the Universal Sound Module (Figure 0.8). What's that? Well it's a very useful GM compatible

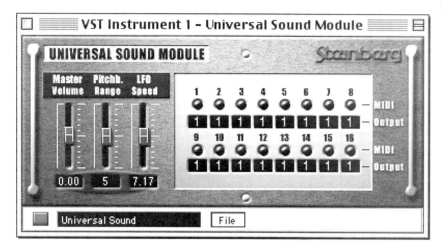

Figure 0.8

Info

The Universal Sound Module is not included with the Cubase SX demo.

software synth. Where is it? Ah! now that's a well kept secret. It was first included with Cubase 5 and is also included with SX/SL. For some reason though, Steinberg seem reluctant to tell anybody about it. A VST Instrument, it can be loaded in the normal way (Figure 0.9). It features four stereo outputs. These are particularly useful for routing sounds to different send effects, such as reverb, in the Mixer.

Figure 0.9

VST Instruments and plug-ins

Many of the projects make use of the VST Instruments and Plug-ins. Because they will be used on computers with widely differing processing power, extensive use of these has been avoided. Usually, only a few are operating at one time.

You can monitor the processing power being used in the VST Performance window [Devices > VST Performance] and if you experience problems, disable the least important plug-in currently in use (Figure 0.10).

OK, that's it. Now Get Creative.

Figure 0.10 VST Performance window

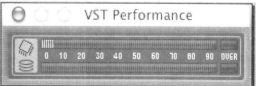

MIDI sequencing: make it easy on yourself

F reddie is frustrated. For over an hour, as part of a college assignment, he's been slaving away on his MIDI keyboard, attempting to record a piano part into Cubase. Trouble is, Fred's main instrument is guitar and although he has a basic knowledge of reading music, his keyboard skills leave a lot to be desired. The piece is only eight measures long and in a simple rock style but each time he does a 'take' there is always something wrong. Sometimes it's out of time, other times it contains bum notes. 'I could be here all day', he thinks, 'and still not get it right'.

I know how he feels. It's a common myth that you have to be a good keyboard player to succeed at arranging and composing. My main instruments are clarinet and saxophone, and I too, am a 'technically challenged' piano player! However, I do manage to write a great deal of music despite my lack of technique. It was a problem until powerful sequencer programs such as Cubase SX/SL appeared on the scene. Now I can actually play the music I write! You can do the same. Here are a few pointers, but first an analogy.

Freddie is practising a transcribed guitar solo and encounters a difficult passage containing some awkward licks. What does he do? (No, he doesn't give up and play a 12 bar blues instead!) He slows the tempo down to a manageable speed, homes in on the nasty bits, and practises those parts repeatedly until he can play them properly. He then puts it all together again, increases the speed and performs a blistering solo. Well that's the theory anyway!

We can apply these principles to the sequencing of piano, or for that matter, any other instrument within Cubase SX/SL.

Slow it down

If you can't play it then slow it down. Why struggle? Computers don't make everything in life easy (the opposite is often the case) but they certainly help us dodgy piano players! However, there is a drawback to playing at a slow tempo, and that's accuracy of timing. Fortunately, quantisation comes to the rescue if that's a problem. More on this in a moment.

Suppose you are recording a piece with Cubase at 120 bpm (beats per minute) and you come up against a passage that you can't play at that speed.

Follow these steps:

1   Scroll the tempo on the Transport panel – disable Master first – to something more comfortable, 90 bpm maybe (Figure 1.1).
2   Record the tricky bit.
3   When you're done, scroll the tempo back to 120 bpm, or activate the Master button (Figure 1.2).

Figure 1.1 Slow the tempo

Break it down

This is very important. Why play large chunks of music and get it repeatedly wrong? Make good use of all this technology. Break the music down into manageable chunks. An eight bar section can very easily be recorded in two four bar sections or even smaller. It is important though, particularly if the material is melodic, to identify phrases, and record them intact where possible. This will help you avoid any loss of continuity and 'feel' that may be lost through recording this way.

   If the music is of a rhythmic character you will probably be able to break things down into significantly smaller segments. Only where necessary of course. Don't overdo it and actually increase your working time. The main purpose of all this is to get things done quickly and easily.

Figure 1.2 Increase the tempo

Cycle record

One of the most useful things about recording in Cubase SX/SL is the option to record in a cycle – a loop. The ability to continuously repeat a tricky part and over-dub piece by piece inside the cycle, adding more music on each lap is invaluable. Again this is akin to the way we practise difficult sections on our instruments. The loop can be set up by:

1   Positioning the left and right locator position.
2   Activating the Cycle button on the Transport panel. (Figure 1.3).

Figure 1.3 Cycle button

Info

There are various options when using Cycle Record. Perhaps the most useful is the combination of Rec Mode set to Normal (overdubs are merged on each pass until you stop recording – however, when you resume recording a new Part is created which overlaps first) and the Cycle Rec set to Mix on the Transport panel (Figure 1.4). Using it this way avoids erasing the music on each pass.

Figure 1.4 Record mode, normal – cycle record, mix

Tip

When cycle recording and quantisation are used together there is a danger of double notes caused by recording events twice. These not only sound strange but can cause problems on some synthesisers. Fortunately, they can be easily erased. [MIDI > Functions > Delete Doubles] (Figure 1.5)

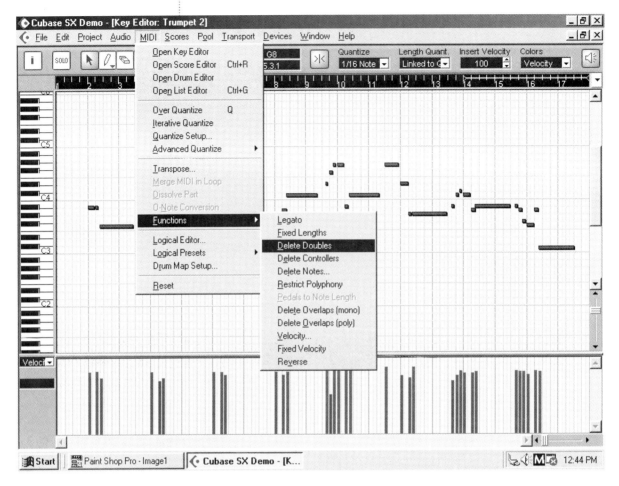

Figure 1.5 Deleting doubled notes.

To quantise or not to quantise

Musicians argue endlessly over this. There's no doubt that quantisation helps tremendously to tighten up loosely played performances. On the other hand it can render a beautifully expressive performance completely lifeless. So when do you resort to quantisation? Well, suppose you are composing techno music as background music for a science documentary video. In this case quantisation is probably a must. Computer music by its very nature lends itself to this kind of treatment. On the other hand, if you were working on music of a romantic nature, for a chocolate box selection advert, the music would need to 'breathe' in a rubato fashion. In this case quantisation would be used sparingly, if at all.

Those are two extremes and there are many styles of music and combinations of instruments which fall in between. Choices have to be made.

Editing – get rid of the bum notes!

We all make mistakes and one of the beauties of Cubase SX/SL is the ability to edit any mistakes and wrong notes after recording. If you've followed the principles outlined above, hopefully, there will not be too many.

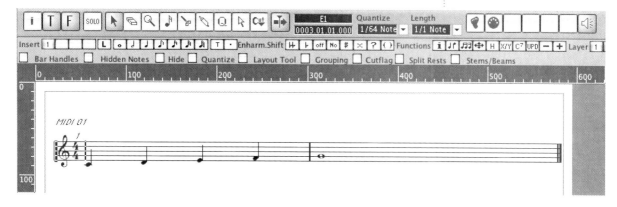

Those of you familiar with conventional music notation will find it easiest to alter, delete, and replace wrong notes in the Score Editor [MIDI > Open Score Editor] (Figure 1.6). Others may prefer the Key Editor [MIDI > Open Key Editor] where you will find a graphic representation of the recording with the notes placed on a grid (Figure 1.7). It's easy to determine the pitch from the virtual keyboard on the left hand side. For detailed use of these Editors, refer to your Cubase SX/SL manual.

Figure 1.6 Score Editor view.

Figure 1.7 Key Editor view.

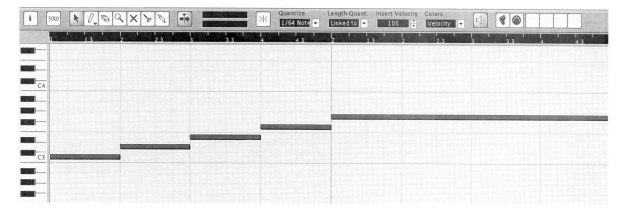

OK, enough talking. It's time for action. In the next chapter, by recording a simple rock and roll piano score you will become familiar with the basic techniques of sequencing and some of the most frequently used functions and tools within Cubase SX/SL.

Project 1: Some rock 'n' roll piano

Musical objectives

- Record a simple rock 'n' roll piano part; length eight bars.

Cubase SX/SL skills

- Recording, cutting and pasting MIDI events and parts in the Project window.
- Toggling between the Master Tempo and a suggested user tempo for ease of playing.
- Quantize selected parts using Iterative Quantize.

Preparation

1 From the CD, copy the folder named 'project 1' to your desktop.
2 Inside the 'project 1' folder you'll find a file named 'template1.cpr'. Open it and use it for this project.
3 Create a folder in which to save your own files as you work through the project.

Info

The template has a time signature of 4/4 and the tempo is 100 bpm. If that's too fast for you, deactivate the Master button on the Transport panel and slow the tempo before you record.

Before you start, return to the project 1 folder on your desktop. Inside you'll find a file called 1.3.cpr. It's the finished thing. Have a listen and view the score (Figure P1.1). This will help those of you still developing your music reading skills to get the gist of it.

Take 1

Track 2: Grand Pno – lh.
Quantize Selector: 1/8 Note.
Inspector: [out: GM] [ch: 2] [prg: 1].
Transport panel: (L) 1.01.01. (R) 5.01.01.

R&R Piano Score

Figure P1.1 Rock 'n' roll piano score.

Figure P1.2 (above) The left hand piano part.

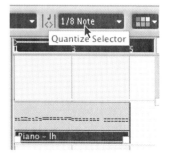

Figure P1.3 (left) The left hand piano part, Key Editor view.

Follow these steps:

1 Record the first four bars of the left hand part (Figure P1.2 and P1.3). You don't have to use your left hand only. This is not a piano lesson! Use both hands if it makes it easier. I do. (If you're not sure how it goes, you may prefer to open 1.1.cpr from the project 1 folder and listen through before you begin recording).

2 Listen back at the master tempo (100 bpm) with the Master button activated. The chances are – depending on your keyboard playing – that it will sound a bit ragged. Mine did! No matter. You can quantize it. Our quantize value is set to 1/8 Note (Figure P1.4). Select the part you have just recorded and choose Over Quantize [MIDI > Over Quantize].

Figure P1.4 Quantize value 1/8 Note on the Toolbar.

3 Listen back again. It should now be rock solid. Selecting Over Quantize has moved all the notes recorded to the nearest eighth note. However, rock 'n' roll piano is often just a little loose so:

4 This time select Iterative Quantize [MIDI > Iterative Quantize]. This type of quantizing moves the notes towards the closest quantize value. How much the notes are moved, and what is considered 'already close to the Quantize value', is set using the 'Iterative Strength' and 'Non Quantize' values in the Quantize Set-up box [MIDI > Quantize Set-up…] (Figure P1.5). Use an 'Iterative Strength' of 60% and leave 'Non Quantize' at 0, the default setting.

Figure P1.5 The Quantize Set-up box.

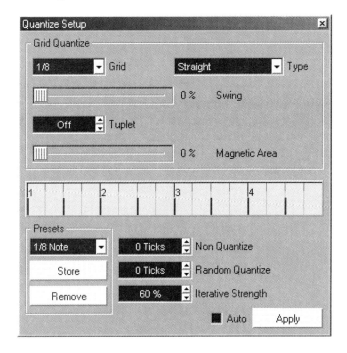

Save Project – compare with 1.1.cpr.

Take 2

Track 1: Grand Pno – rh.
Quantize Selector: 1/8 Note.
Inspector: [out: GM] [ch: 1] [prg: 1].
Transport panel: (L) 1.01.01. (R) 5.01.01.

1 Now record the first four bars of the right hand piano part (Figures P1.6 and P1.7). If it's difficult to play, try playing the two harmonies separately on different passes.

Right Hand

Figure P1.6 The right hand piano part.

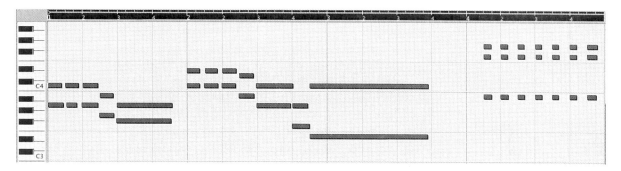

2 Listen back at 100 bpm and, if necessary, apply Iterative Quantize.

Figure P1.7 The right hand piano part, Key Editor view.

I expect you have noticed that bars 5, 6 and 7 in the left hand part are the same as bars 1, 2 and 3. To save time (and possibly high blood pressure, depending on your piano playing skills), copy those bars to bar 5.

3 With the Project cursor at 4.01.01 use the Scissors tool to split the part.
4 Select the first three bars (1-4). Copy and paste them to bar 5. Alternatively, select the first three bars (1-4) and duplicate the new part to bar 5 by dragging it. (Click, hold and drag while pressing Alt on your computer keyboard).
5 The right hand part follows the same pattern so repeat the above procedure on that part too.

Save project – compare with 1.2.cpr.

Tip

When pasting a copied part, make sure the project cursor is set to the exact destination you require otherwise it will end up somewhere else! Bar 999 perhaps! It happens.

Take 3

1 Return to track 2, set the locators between 8.01.01 and 9.01.01 and record the last bar of the left hand piano part (Figures P1.8 and P1.9).

Left Hand

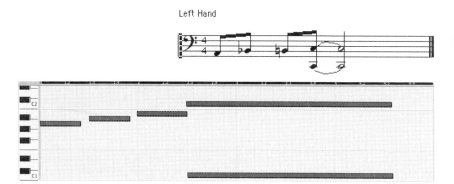

Figure P1.8 The left hand piano part, bar 8.

Figure P1.9 The left hand piano part, bar 8, Key Editor view.

2 Switch to track 1 and record the last bar of the right hand piano part (Figures P1.10 and P1.11). If necessary, apply Iterative Quantize to both and you're done.

Figure P1.10 The right hand piano part, bar 8.

Right Hand

Figure P1.11 The right hand piano part, bar 8, Key Editor view.

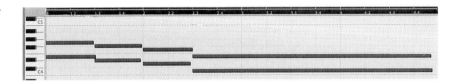

3 Save project – compare with 1.3.cpr.

Get real with MIDI

As part of a college assignment, Sara has been sequencing classical music, a string quartet, with Cubase. She has played all the parts correctly from her MIDI keyboard, but for some reason, the overall result is less than convincing. The instruments just don't sound realistic.

This is a common scenario. Of course it's well nigh impossible to recreate the performance of a real violinist, or come to that, any other instrumentalist, but a pretty convincing job can be made of it if you approach things the right way. You may not be able to fool musicians but you can certainly produce something worthy enough for many a multimedia project. However, there is much to learn to achieve a good result.

So how do you transform your Cubase SX/SL projects into something that sounds like the London Philharmonic Orchestra or, for that matter, something by Jimi Hendrix? By using your imagination, of course. Whether you have a top of the range sound module or just a humble Sound Blaster Audigy card, you'll not get far without it.

Forget the keyboard and concentrate on the virtual instrument you are recording. If it's a violin, imagine yourself actually playing it. Be that violinist. You are bowing those short rhythmic stop notes, those long flowing melodies that string sections are so good at. The same applies to any instrument. Try to get inside the mind of your virtual musician. Before you can do this confidently, you will have to spend time listening.

Listen and learn

Listen to all kinds of music. To earn a crust arrangers and composers must be able to write in just about any style. If you can afford it, get out and attend live music events and hear as much variation of style as possible. Classical – old and contemporary – jazz, rock, folk, in fact just about anything. These day's there's a wealth of recorded material available on the Internet in all styles, old and new. Select the good stuff (legal of course) and download it. You don't have to like all this music but you should absorb it. It will all resurface when you need it.

Learn how to listen

There's not much point in listening to all this music if you haven't learned how to listen. Instead of just listening to the overall sound picture, train your ear to single out the instruments from orchestras, groups and bands. Identify the musical families they belong to.

Was that an oboe or a cor anglais solo? Is that a viola or violin playing those low notes? Is he playing a fretless bass guitar or just a regular electric bass? Are those trombones or French horns in that quiet orchestral passage? Is that a tenor or alto saxophone break in that jazz rock number?

These are the kinds of questions you should ask yourself. This is easy in a live situation, but considerably harder with recorded music. Pay particular attention to the way these instruments are played, both in a solo situation and as part of a section. It's also important to understand the comfortable playing range of the various instruments.

Get a life! – play with others

Working with Cubase SX/SL provides a wonderful virtual environment but unfortunately it's usually a solitary one. As well as listening, there is no substitute for actually playing live, in rock bands, jazz bands, wind bands, orchestras, folk groups and so on. The list is endless. This provides invaluable first hand experience of how real instruments are played. If you can, have a go at some of these instruments. (Ask first of course!)

Sequencing examples

I mentioned earlier how important it is to use our imagination when playing what are, after all, imaginary instruments. OK, they are samples of real instruments, but lifeless unless you know how to use them. Here are some pointers.

Sequencing woodwinds and brass

The woodwinds, in the main, are split into two groups, reed instruments – clarinets, oboe, cor anglais (English horn), bassoons, saxophones – and flutes, recorders and piccolos. The brass are comprised mainly of trumpets, trombones, horns, and tuba. It's important to remember that woodwind and brass players need to breathe! I've heard many a woodwind part ruined by a virtuoso keyboard player who has not thought about this. Be careful not to create overlaps when playing from the keyboard. If it happens, (Figure 2.1) clean them up, from within whichever Editor window you are using, with MIDI > Functions > Delete Overlaps mono/poly (Figure 2.2).

Figure 2.1 Overlapping notes.

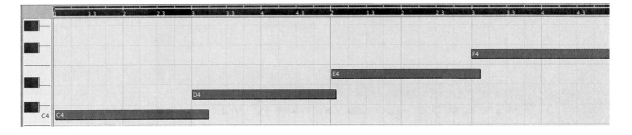

Bear in mind that 'blowers' articulate with their tongues. Unless a passage is deliberately slurred there should be small gaps between notes. This is sometimes

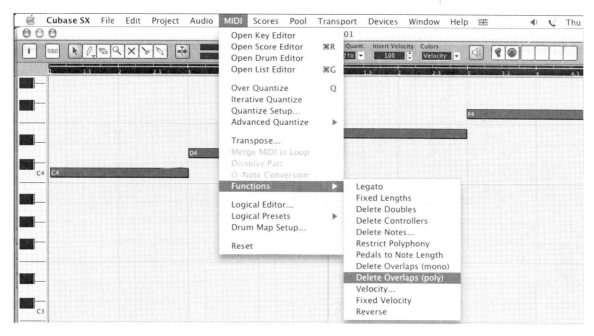

Figure 2.2 Overlapping notes fixed.

difficult to achieve and a bit of a fiddle but it's usually a matter of keeping the best take and polishing it up afterwards, in either the Score or Key Editors. Here are two interpretations of a short flute solo (Figure 2.3).

Figure 2.3 Flute solo.

Mozart Symphony No.40

Follow these steps:

- Load getreal/flutes/badflt.cpr.
- Set the MIDI output to your GM sound source.

The flute here is badly played and ignores the breath mark (V) in the fourth measure as well as the articulation marks (slurs and staccato).

- Load getreal/flutes/goodflt.cpr.
- Set the MIDI output to your GM sound source.

This is clearly much better and pays heed to the articulation as well as a gap for that all important breath.

Saxophone solos will require subtle use of pitch bend to make them sound at all convincing. This is best done whilst playing, using the pitch bend controller on the MIDI keyboard. Pitch bend can be added afterwards but it's hard to beat the spontaneity of adding it live. Vibrato is sometimes used by sax players and this can be achieved with a touch of modulation. Go easy though, to avoid that 'nanny goat' sax sound!

Info

To examine the Cubase SX/SL project files for this chapter, copy the folder named 'getreal' from the CD to your computer.

- Load getreal/alto/hodges.cpr.
- Set the MIDI output to your GM sound source.

This is a short solo in the style of the late Johnny Hodges, famed for his beautiful tone and incredible note bending. Well I can't guarantee the tone – this is a synthetic sax after all – but I have managed to emulate his playing style with the use of pitch bend.

You can inspect the pitch bend and modulation data in the List Editor [MIDI > Open List Editor] (Figure 2.4).

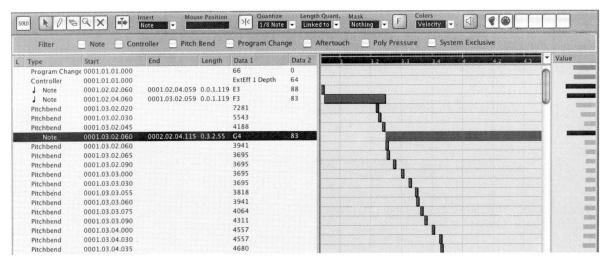

Figure 2.4 Pitch bend data, List Editor view.

Another way to view the pitch bend information is in the Key Editor. Have a look [MIDI > Open Key Editor]. Click on the arrow (Figure 2.5) just below the keyboard, on the lower-left side of the screen. A menu appears (Figure 2.6). Choose Pitch Bend and a graphic representation appears in the controller display. Pitch bend can be drawn and edited here using the Pencil (Figure 2.7).

Figure 2.5 Click on the arrow.

Figure 2.6 The controller menu.

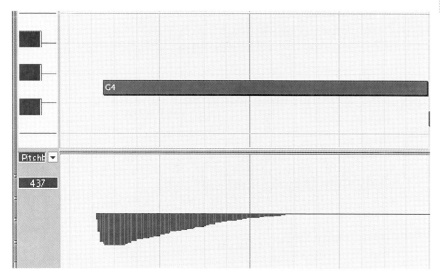

Figure 2.7 Pitch bend, controller display.

Tip

Need to edit more than one controller in either the Key Editor or Drum Editor at the same time? Right-click in the display area (control and click on a Mac) and select 'Create new controller lane' from the Quick menu to add more lanes (Figure 2.8).

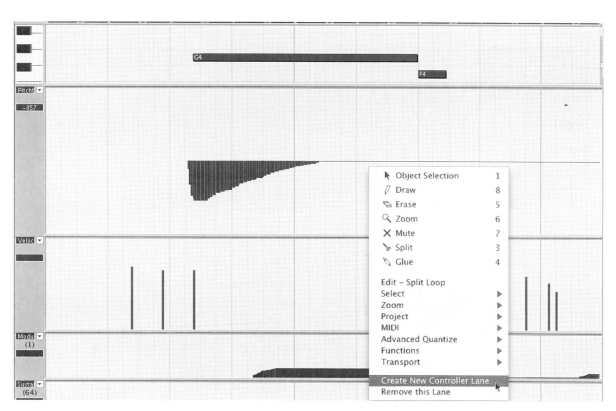

Figure 2.8 Controller Lanes and Quick menu.

Sequencing strings

The conventional string orchestra uses four instruments. The violin, viola, cello and bass.

When emulating the instruments of the string orchestra it is important to distinguish between legato playing (long bowed sections) and individually bowed notes. As with the wind instruments, small gaps between individual notes are best, so try to adapt your playing style for this. To capture those long flowing lines it's probably best to select the notes required in the Score or Key Editors and apply Legato [MIDI > Functions > Legato] (Figure 2.9).

Figure 2.9 Applying Legato.

Figure 2.10 Legato strings.

Here's an example (Figure 2.10):

Follow these steps:

- Load getreal/strings/okstrings.cpr.
- Set the MIDI output to your GM sound source.

This sequence has been played accurately enough, but the legato phrases remain choppy.

- Load getreal/strings//lgstrngs.cpr.
- Set the MIDI output to your GM sound source.

In this version Legato has been applied. It's better, don't you think? All the notes line up end to end and the result is more authentic sounding. Check them in the Key Editor.

Sequencing drums and percussion

Many Cubase SX/SL users prefer to sequence their drum parts by entering the beats using the Drum Editor. This is fine for music that relies heavily on drum loops such as dance music. Others prefer to play a 'virtual kit'. It depends on the style of music. If dynamic variation and a live feel is required it's probably best to play the part first and edit it afterwards in one of the Editors. If a repetitive loop is needed, step entry may be the way to go.

For 'live style drums', here are a few pointers:

- Another myth: 'Drums underpin the track so you have to record them first'. Not so. Unless the music is loop based – in which case they will probably be entered step by step anyway – it's often best to record some melodic material first. The advantage of this is that you will be playing with the other parts. All the dynamic variation and feel of the other parts will influence how you play the 'virtual drum kit' and will help instil feel into the music.
- If possible record in stretches of eight bars or so at a time. This helps create a natural flow and is preferable to cutting and pasting one or two bar segments.

- Drum rolls are often best sequenced by step entry. It's no easy matter to roll two fingers as fast as two drum sticks. This is usually done in the Drum Editor.
- On a conventional kit, try playing the kick and snare drums first and overdub the hi-hats, cymbals and toms afterwards on separate tracks.

To illustrate how this might be done, I've recorded a four bar rock groove with a fill in the fourth bar.

- Load getreal/drums/groove.cpr.
- Set the MIDI output to your GM sound source.

It was done in three stages:

1 I laid down the kick drum and snare together for three bars and left the fourth bar blank. Drums are perhaps the hardest instrument to play accurately from a MIDI keyboard – that's my excuse anyway – so, I set a value of sixteen (1/16 Note) and used Iterative Quantize to tighten things up a bit.
2 I moved to a different track, and added the hi-hat figure again using Iterative Quantize.
3 I then moved to a third track and recorded the fill on toms with a cymbal crash thrown in for good measure.

Having the drums separated like this also makes it easier to carry out editing procedures. Examine the sequences in the Score, Key and Drum Editors (Figures 2.11, 2.12 and 2.13). For an overall picture select all the parts. Check that the GM map is selected for all three tracks in the Inspector.

Figure 2.11 Drum sequences, Score Editor view.

Figure 2.12 Drum sequences, Key Editor view.

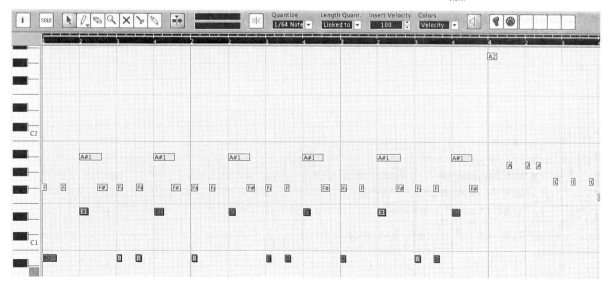

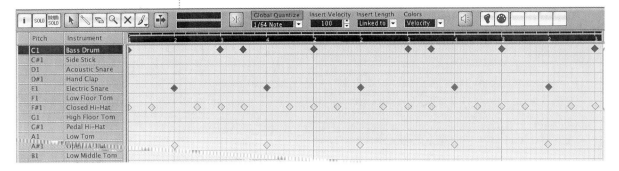

Figure 2.13 Drum sequences, Drum Editor view.

> ### Tip
>
> Avoid playing three things on the same beat – apart from the kick drum – because drummers don't possess three arms and it may sound unnatural.

Sequencing guitars

How you approach this depends on whether the instrument is acoustic or electric and whether the music is melodic or rhythmic. Straightforward melodic lines are quite easy with nylon string, steel string and jazz guitars but judicious use of pitch bend will often be needed. Rock guitar lines are harder. More pitch bend is usually required. Modulation can be added afterwards on a separate track and is one way to simulate a real player's use of vibrato. Take care not to overdo it though.

Follow these steps:

- Load getreal/gtr/lick.cpr to hear a short lick recorded this way.
- Set the MIDI output to your GM sound source.

Use the List and Key Editors to examine the pitch bend and modulation information. Figure 2.14 shows the modulation, recorded separately on track 2.

Figure 2.14 Controller display, modulation.

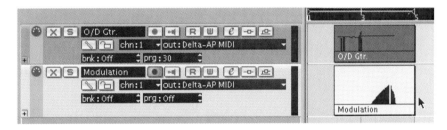

Rhythm guitars need to be approached carefully. Although a real guitar has six strings, things can get very muddy if you try to faithfully reproduce this with a synthesised MIDI guitar. You will also use up valuable polyphony and on a busy sequence this could result in the unexpected drop out of notes on other instruments.

Try using less notes in a chord. Real guitarists do not always use all six strings anyway. Often, only three notes are needed if the guitar is used in the background. Open spacing can give the illusion of depth. For example, a chord of C major – C3, E3, G3 (Figures 2.15a and 2.15b) could be played as G2, E3, C4.

Figure 2.15a Chord spacing.

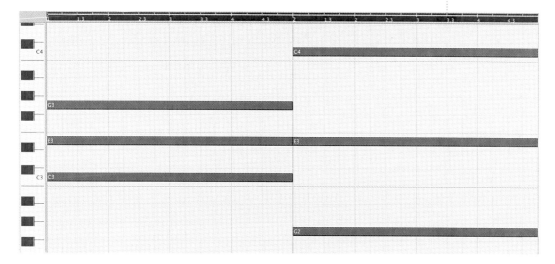

Figure 2.15b Chord spacing, Key Editor view.

'But what about seventh chords' I hear you say. Omit the fifth or the root but keep the third. How you move from chord to chord depends very much on voice leading and is a vast subject beyond the scope of this book.

Guitar players can of course use a special MIDI interface to play in their parts. This could be useful for playing bass, string and horn parts and other monophonic instruments but the guitar itself would be best recorded on an audio track.

Quantisation

Cubase SX/SL provides plenty of scope here. How you approach it depends mainly on the instrument you are imitating and the style of music. Choosing a quantize value in the Quantize Selector will move all the notes played to the nearest division of the beat. For example; selecting 1/8 Note will move things to the nearest eighth note, 1/16 Note to the nearest sixteenth note and so on.

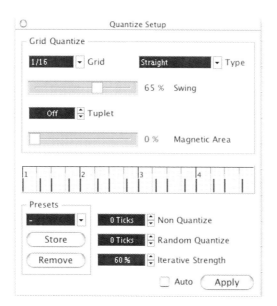

Figure 2.16 Quantize Setup dialogue.

Standard quantisation is fine for many uses but if a less rigid result is required you can further adjust the values in the Quantize Setup dialogue (Figure 2.16). Here's a quick run-down of the main functions:

1 *Grid value and type* – where you select basic note values for quantizing. Using these menus amounts to the same thing as using the Quantize Selector on the Toolbar, in the Project window.
2 *The Swing Slider* – adjusting this slider will create a swing or shuffle feel by offsetting every second note (eighth, sixteenth or whatever Type is selected) on the Grid.
3 *Magnetic Area* – where only specified notes, within a certain distance from the grid, are affected. A slider and percentage values are used to define the area.

When and how much to quantize depends mainly on the musical material being sequenced. For example, you may be recording a flowing string melody. In this case quantisation is best avoided. However if it's a rhythmic 'marcato' string part then some quantisation may be appropriate. After all real string players are often behind the beat. Only joking! (time to duck).

Here's an example. A three piece horn section – trumpet, tenor saxophone and baritone saxophone – recorded as MIDI instruments into Cubase can be very accurately played but somehow still sound imprecise when recorded without quantisation.

Follow these steps:

1 Load getreal/horns/horns.cpr.
2 Set the MIDI output to your GM sound source.
3 Have a listen. What do you think? Examine the sequences in the Score Editor and you will see that they are all played accurately enough. What do I think? OK I suppose, but I'd want better than that if was hiring them! View the sequences in the Key Editor and things don't look so tight.
4 Listen to getreal/horns/hornsqua.cpr. Quantisation was used and things are very much improved because the actual note lengths are left unchanged but they all start at exactly the same time. This retains the sense of 'realness' and is close to how a brass section actually plays. In fact I have achieved exactly what most 'real' horn sections strive for! But now they lack feeling and sound a bit mechanical. A quick way to loosen things up without spoiling the tight feel would be to randomise the notes by a few ticks in the Track Parameters. A similar effect can be achieved by applying Iterative Quantize to a recorded part. Depending on how this is set up, only certain notes are moved. It can be progressively applied until the required degree of tightness is heard.
5 Listen to getreal/horns/hornsit.cpr. That's more like it. The cheques are in the post!

Dynamics

A fine musical performance, whatever the genre, usually contains a degree of dynamic variation. It goes without saying that a MIDI sequence that emulates such a performance must also contain the same dynamic ingredients; volume (loud or soft) gradual changes of volume (crescendo and diminuendo) sudden changes of

volume (sforzando) and accented notes. Three MIDI controllers are used dynami-
cally in Cubase SX/SL – Volume, Expression and Velocity.

Velocity controls the volume of an individual note depending on how hard or soft
a key is struck on your MIDI keyboard. Again imagination is needed. Remember,
be that percussionist. Take this timpani figure for example. (Figure 2.17)

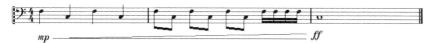

Figure 2.17 Timpani figure.

Follow these steps:

- Load getreal/timpani/timpani.cpr.
- Set the MIDI output to your GM sound source.
- Listen and examine the sequence in the Key Editor with Velocity selected in the
  controller display (Figure 2.18). You will notice that the velocity values start at
  55 and end at 125. The gradual increase in attack is not exact, nor would it be
  if played by a real percussionist. Although Velocity values can be used to
  control volume and fade outs it is wiser to use Volume and Expression.

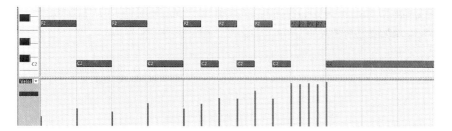

Figure 2.18 Timpani velocity.

Volume (Controller No. 7) and Expression (Controller No. 11) are essentially the
same thing. They both control the volume of a sequence. However, when export-
ing your work as a MIDI file for use on another computer, keyboard or sound module, it is best to use Volume as a master function, to control the overall picture, and
Expression for the dynamic changes within that picture. This allows the end user to
adjust the balance of individual instruments on their equipment (what sounds loud
on your gear may sound quiet on theirs) without spoiling the dynamic content of
the recorded data.

A foot pedal (much like on a real piano) can be used to control these parameters in real time when playing from a keyboard. Being the imperfect keyboard player that I am, I prefer to add these changes afterwards by either using the Mixer, or
the Key and List Editors.

Project 2: a rock score

Musical objectives

- Sequence a rock score comprised of piano, guitar, bass guitar and drums.
- Achieve a realistic interpretation of a live rock band.

Cubase SX/SL skills

- Loading a Cubase SX/SL VST Instrument.
- Using the LM-7 Drum Kit
- Entering beats in the Drum Editor
- Viewing Mapped Drums in the Score Editor
- Setting Volume, Pan and Velocity settings in the Inspector
- Using Transpose in the Inspector

Preparation

Info

The template has a time signature of 4/4 and the tempo is 100 bpm. If that's too fast for you, deactivate the Master button on the Transport panel and slow the tempo before you record.

1 From the CD, copy the folder named 'project 2' to your desktop.
2 Inside the 'project 2' folder you'll find a file named 'template2.cpr.' Open it and use it for this project.
3 Create a folder in which to save your own files as you work through the project.

If your music reading skills are not too hot, don't be put off by the score (Figure P2.1 and P2.2). From the project 2 folder, load 2.11.cpr – the finished thing – and have a listen.

Play it through several times and practise reading the score one instrument at a time. When you are familiar with the tune, work through the project.

Take 1

Track 2: Grand Pno – lh.
Quantize Selector: 1/8 Note
Inspector: [out: GM] [chn: 2] [prg: 1]
Transport panel: (L) 1.01.01. (R) 5.01.01.

Page 1

It's Closing Time

Figure P2.1
The score, page 1.

Page 2

Figure P2.2
The score, page 2.

Follow these steps:

1 Record the first four bars of the left hand piano part (Figure P2.3 and P2.4). Yes, you've guessed it. It's the same four bars used in project 1 (Figures P1.4 and P1.5). If you want, copy and paste them over.

Figure P2.3 The left hand piano part.

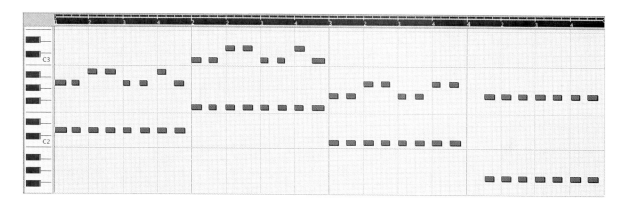

2 Listen back. If you slowed it down, activate the Master button on the Transport panel to listen at the correct tempo. If it's not as tight as you would like apply Iterative Quantize repeatedly until you're happy.

3 Save Project – compare with 2.1.cpr.

Figure P2.4 The left hand piano part, Key Editor view.

Take 2

Track 1: Grand Pno – lh.
Quantize Selector: 1/8 Note.
Inspector: [out: GM] [chn: 1] [prg: 1].
Transport panel: (L) 1.01.01. (R) 5.01.01.

Follow these steps:

1 Now record the first four bars of the right hand piano part (Figures P2.5 and P2.6). Again it's the same four bars used in project 1 (P1.8 and P1.9). If you want, copy and paste them over.

Figure P2.5 The right hand piano part.

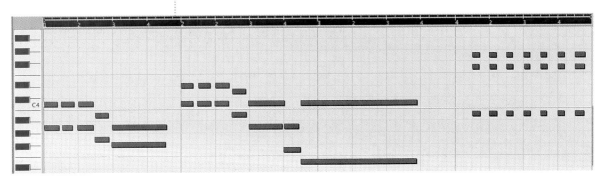

Figure P2.6
The right hand piano part, Key Editor view.

2 Listen back and apply Iterative Quantize until you're satisfied with the result.

3 Save Song – compare with 2.2.cpr.

Take 3

Figure P2.7 The left hand piano part, bars 5-9.

1 Return to track 2, set the locators to (L) 5.01.01 (R) 9.01.01 and record the next four bars of the left hand piano part (Figures P2.7 and P2.8).

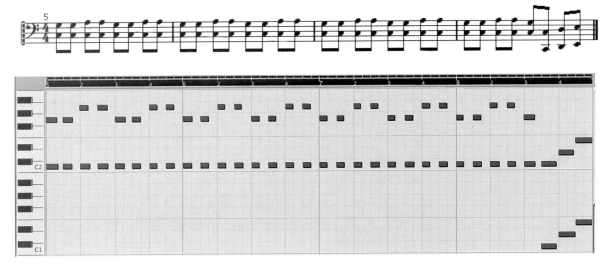

Figure P2.8 The left hand piano part, bars 5-9, Key Editor view.

2 Switch to track 1 and record the right hand piano part between the same locator set up (Figures P2.9 and P2.10).

3 Listen back and as before, apply Iterative Quantize until happy.

4 Save Project – compare with 2.3.cpr.

Figure P2.9 (above) The right hand piano part, bars 5-9.   **Figure P2.10 (below)** The right hand piano part, bars 5-9, Key Editor view.

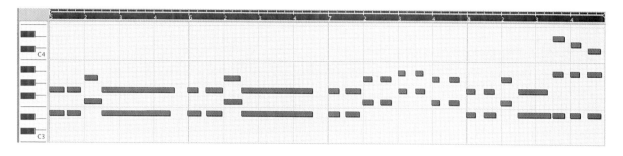

Take 4

1   Return to track 2, set the locators at (L) 9.01.01 (R) 13.01.01 and record the next four bars of the left hand piano part (Figures P2.11 and P2.12).

Figure P2.11 The left hand piano part, bars 9-13.

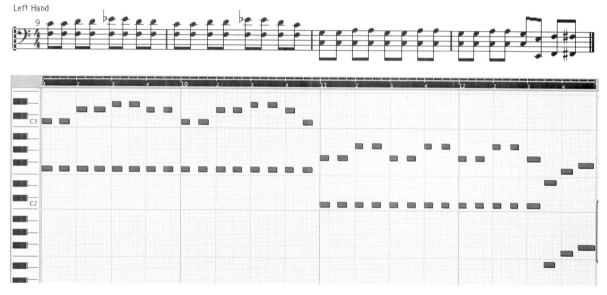

2   Switch to track 1 and record the right hand piano part between the same locator set up (Figures P2.13 and P2.14).

Figure P2.12 The left hand piano part, bars 9-13, Key Editor view.

Figure P2.13 (above) The right hand piano part, bars 9-13.   **Figure P2.14 (below)** The right hand piano part, bars 9-13, Key Editor view.

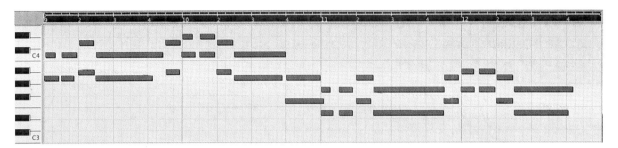

3 Listen back and once again, apply Iterative Quantize to both parts.

4 Save Project – compare with 2.4.cpr.

Take 5

Figure P2.15 The left hand piano part, bars 13-17.

1 Return to track 2, set the locators to (L) 13.01.01 (R) 17.01.1 and record the next four bars of the left hand part (Figures P2.15 and P2.16).

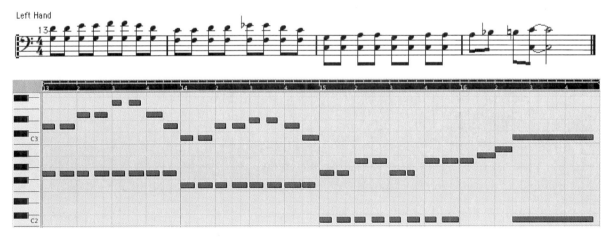

Figure P2.16 The left hand piano part, bars 13-17, Key Editor view.

2 Switch to track 1 and record the right hand piano part between the same locator set up (Figures P2.17 and P2.18).

Figure P2.17 (above) The right hand piano part, bars 13-17.   **Figure P2.18 (below)** The right hand piano part, bars 13-17, Key Editor view.

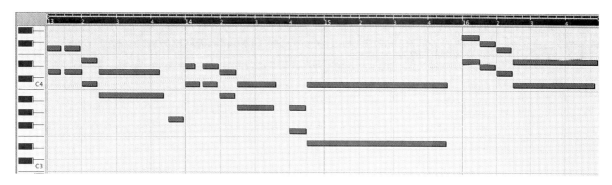

3 Listen back and tweak the quantize parameters for both sequences.
4 Save Project – compare with 2.5.cpr.

OK, that's the piano out of the way. Now for the guitar. Take a look at the guitar part on the score (Figures P2.1and P2.2). You'll notice that it's in two part harmony. No doubt a real guitarist would have played a few more notes, but for our purposes it's fine. I chose the GM MIDI pre-set 31, Distortion Guitar for extra bite.

Take 6

Track 3: Dist. Guitar.
Quantize Selector: 1/8 Note.
Inspector: [out: GM] [chn: 3] [prg: 31].
Transport panel: (L) 5.01.01. (R) 9.01.01.

Follow these steps:

Figure P2.19 The guitar part, bars 5-9.

1 Record the fours bars between the locators (Figures P2.19 and P2.20).

Figure P2.20 (below) Key Editor view.

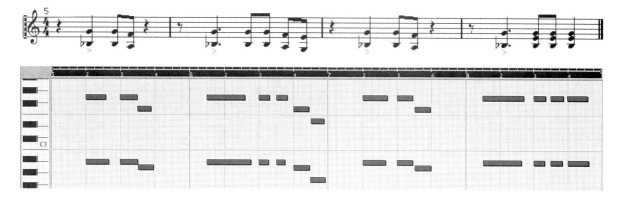

Figure P2.21 The guitar part, bars 9-13.

2 Record the next four bars, 9-13 (Figures P2.21 and P2.22).

Figure P2.22 The guitar part, bars 9-13, Key Editor view.

3 Record another four bars, 13-17 (Figures P2.23 and P2.24).

4 Listen back and apply Iterative Quantize for all three parts until you are happy with the result.

5 Save Project – compare with 2.6.cpr.

Figure P2.23 The guitar part, bars 13-17.

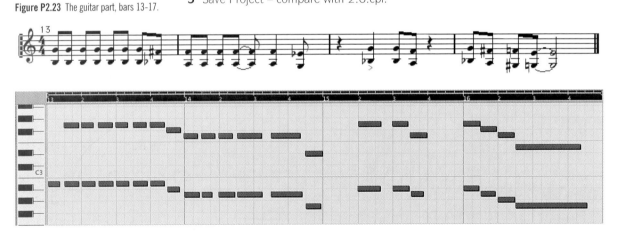

Figure P2.24 The guitar part, bars 13-17, Key Editor view.

For the bass guitar I have chosen the VB-1, one of the VST instruments included with Cubase SX/SL .

Take 7

Track 4: Bass Guitar.
Quantize Selector: 1/8 Note.
Inspector: [out: VB-1] [chn: 4] [prg: Dark Click].
Track Parameters: [Transpose: -12]
Transport panel: (L) 1.01.01. (R) 5.01.01.

Info

Note the transposition of -12 in the Inspector for Take 7 (Track Parameters section). The reason for this? – bass guitar is written one octave higher than it actually sounds.

If you open up the VST Instrument rack [Devices > VST Instruments] you'll see that the VB-1 is loaded, complete with the Dark Click pre-set and all ready to go (Figure P2.25). For further experimentation click on the edit button to reveal the instrument itself (Figure P2.26). I've left the pre-set at the default setting. Go on, do some virtual knob twiddling!

Figure 2.25 The VST Instrument rack.

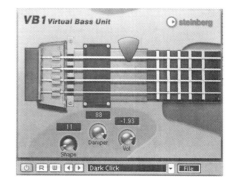

Figure 2.26 The VB-1.

Follow these steps:

1 Record the four bars between the locators (Figures P2.27 and P2.28).

Figure P2.27 The bass guitar part, bars 5-9.

2 Record the next four bars, 9-13 (Figures P2.29 and P2.30).

Figure P2.28 The bass guitar part, bars 5-9, Key Editor view.

Figure P2.29 (above) The bass guitar part, bars 9-13.   **Figure P2.30 (below)** The bass guitar part, bars 9-13, Key Editor view.

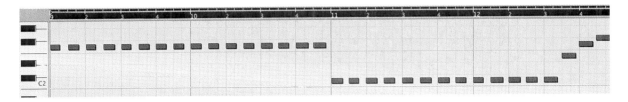

3 Record another four bars, 13-17 (Figures P2.31 and P2.32).

Figure P2.31 (above) The bass guitar part, bars 13-17.   **Figure P2.32 (below)** The bass guitar part, bars 13-17, Key Editor view.

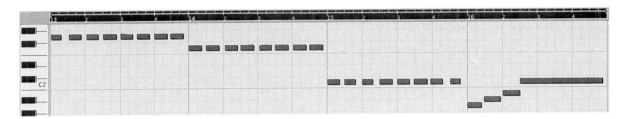

4 Listen back and apply Iterative Quantize for all three parts until you are happy with the result.

5 Save Project – compare with 2.7.cpr

Right, now for the drums. Instead of a GM drum kit use the LM-7 supplied with Cubase SX/SL .

Take 8

Track 5: Kick/Snare dr.
Quantize Selector: 1/8 Note.
Inspector: [out: LM-7] [chn: 10] [prg: Compressor] [map: GM Map].
Transport panel: (L) 5.01.01 (R) 9.01.01.

As with the bass, the LM-7 is already loaded and ready to use. Click on the edit button to reveal the drum machine interface. Experiment with the tone and velocities of individual drum sounds (Figure P2.33).

Figure 2.33 The LM-7

Follow these steps:

1 Play and record the kick and snare drums together (C1 and D1 or E1) between the locators (Figures P2.34 and P2.35).

Figure P2.34 The kick and snare drums, bars 5-9.

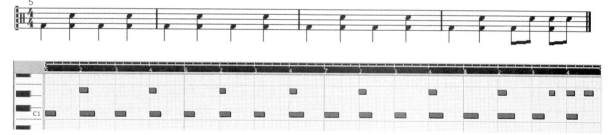

Figure P2.35 The kick and snare drums, bars 5-9, Key Editor view.

2 Listen back and tweak the quantize parameters until a nice rock feel is achieved. If you find it difficult to play kick and snare together record them separately, on separate passes.

3 Save Project – compare with 2.8a.cpr.

Info

Drum parts can be entered manually in the Drum Editor as an alternative method:

1 Select the Kick/Snare track and with the pencil tool, draw a part.
2 Select the newly drawn part and open the Drum Editor [MIDI > Open Drum Editor].
3 Use the Drum Stick tool to enter the beats.

5 The next four bars, 9-13, are the same. You can either record or enter them again or do it the easy way and duplicate the previous part.

6 Play and record, or enter manually, the last four bars, 13-17 (Figures P2.36. P2.37 and P2.38).

7 Apply Iterative Quantize.

8 Save Project – compare with 2.8b.cpr.

Figure P2.36 The kick and snare drums, bars 13-17.

Regardless of the method you used to create the drum sequences in take 8, take a look at the results in all three Edit windows.

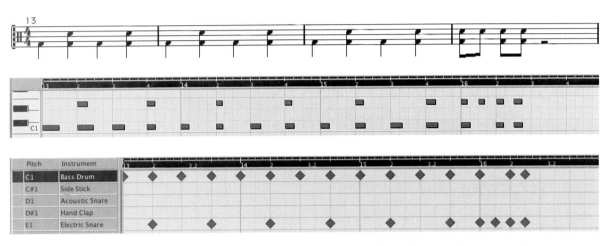

Figure P2.37 The kick and snare drums, bars 13-17, Key Editor and view.

Figure P2.38 Drum Editor view.

> **Tip**
>
> A quick way to create a Part – with the arrow tool, double click between the locators.

• The Drum Editor will provide a graphical display and corresponding drum names – remember to select a GM Drum Map – bottom left corner.

• The Key Editor will provide a graphical display that corresponds to the notes actually played on the keyboard.

• The Score Editor will present the parts as standard drum notation on a special drum staff. If you played it correctly, it should look the same as our score (Figure P2.36). Follow these steps:

1 Select a part and open the Score Editor [MIDI > Open Score Editor].

2 From within the Score Editor open the Staff Settings dialogue box. [Scores > Staff Settings] (Figure P2.39).

3 In the Main section, change the Display Quantize 'Rests' value to 4. Leave the 'Notes' value at 16.

4 Leave 'Auto Quantize' unchecked.

5 In the Interpret. Flags section tick 'Clean Lengths' and 'No Overlap'.

6 In the Presets section, near the bottom, select 'jazz+pop – drum set'.

7 Finally, click the 'Apply' button and voila! – a drum score appears, hopefully!

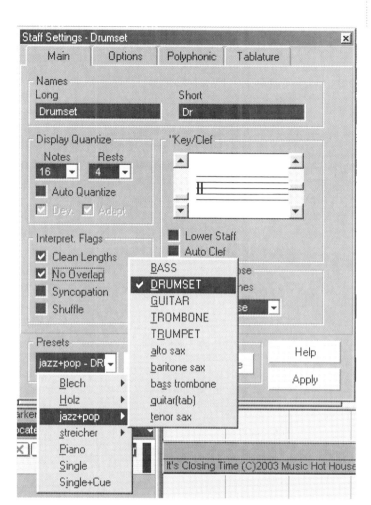

Figure P2.39 The Staff Settings dialogue
box.

Take 9

Track 6: Hi-Hat.
Quantize Selector: 1/8 Note.
Inspector: [out: LM-7] [chn: 10] [prg: Compressor] [map: GM Map].
locators: (L) 5.01.01 (R) 9.01.01.

Follow these steps:

Figure P2.40 The closed hi-hat, bars 5-9.

Figure P2.41 The closed hi-hat, bars 5-9, Key Editor view.

1 Record or manually enter the hi-hat (F#1) between the locators (Figures P2.40, P2.41 and P2.42).

2 Listen back and maybe apply Iterative Quantize.

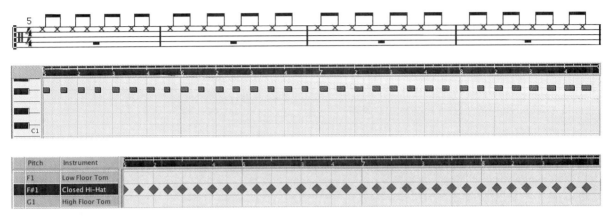

Figure P2.42 Drum Editor view.

3 The next four bars, 9-13, are the same. You can either record or enter them again or do it the easy way and duplicate the previous sequence.

4 Record or enter the hi-hat, bars 13-17 (Figures P2.43, P2.44 and P2.45).

5 Listen back and maybe tweak the quantize parameters.

6 Save Project – compare with 2.9.cpr.

Figure P2.43 The closed hi-hat, bars 13-17.

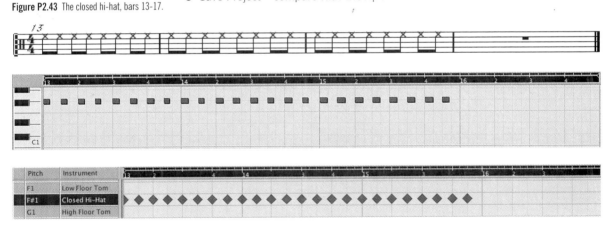

Figure P2.44 The closed hi-hat, bars 13-17, Key Editor view.

Figure P2.45 Drum Editor view.

Take 10

Track 7: Toms.
Quantize Selector: 1/8 Note.
Inspector: [out: LM-7] [chn: 10] [prg: Compressor] [map: GM Map].
Transport panel: (L) 4.01.01 (R) 5.01.01.

Follow these steps:

1 Record both toms together (A1 and C2) or enter them manually in the Drum
   Editor using the GM Drum Set (Figures P2.46, P2.47 and P2.48).
2 Listen back and apply Iterative Quantize.
3 Save Project – compare with 2.10.cpr.

Figure P2.46 The toms.

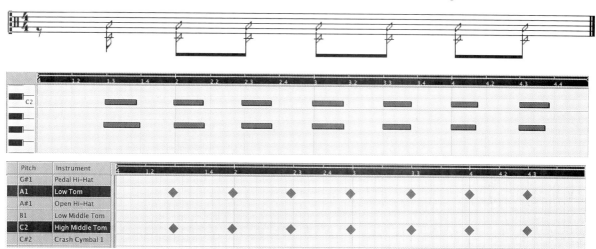

Figure P2.47 The toms, Key Editor view.

Figure P2.48 The toms, Drum Editor view.

Take 11

Track 8: Crash Cymbal.
Quantize Selector: 1/8 Note.
Inspector: [out: LM-7] [chn: 10] [prg: Compressor] [map: GM Map].
Transport panel: (L) 5.01.01 (R) 17.01.01.

Follow these steps:

1 They're not marked on the score, but, as a finishing touch, why not record the odd crash cymbal (C#2). On the first beat of bar 5 maybe. I also placed one at the beginning of bar 9 and another on the fourth 1/8th note in bar 16 (Figures P2.49, P2.50 and P2.51).

Figure P2.49 The cymbal crashes.

Figure P2.50 The cymbal crashes, Key Editor view.

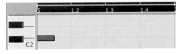

Figure P2.51 The cymbal crashes, Drum Editor view.

2 Listen back and maybe use Iterative Quantize.
3 To achieve a balanced result, I separated the piano (both tracks) and guitar in the stereo picture by panning them slightly left and right in the Inspector. Try it. Leave the bass in the centre. Experiment with the Panorama knob (pan) on the various sounds in the LM-7. Be careful though, a drummer's arms only stretch so far!
4 As for volume this will depend very much on your GM sound source. I have lowered the guitar which sounds rather loud on my GM module. Find your own balance.
5 Save Project – compare with 2.11.cpr.

Project 3: a jazz funk score

Musical objectives

- Achieve a realistic interpretation of a short jazz funk score comprising rhythm and 'horns' – trumpet, tenor sax and trombone.
- Improvise one-bar breaks in the horn parts using a blues scale.
- Achieve a satisfactory mix – volume balance and stereo picture.

Cubase SX/SL skills

- Using Quantize Set-up to configure and apply a swing groove.
- Using the Mixer
- Using the Random section in the Track Parameters to humanise the horn section tracks.

Preparation

1 From the CD, copy the folder named 'project 3' to your desktop.
2 Inside the 'project 3' folder you'll find a file named 'template3.cpr'. Open it and use it for this project.
3 Create a folder in which to save your own files as you work through the project.

OK, take a look at the score (Figures P3.1, P3.2, P3.3 and P3.4). Ouch! It looks complicated, right? Don't be put off. This kind of music looks horrendous written down. Once you hear it things make more sense.

Info

The template has a time signature of 4/4 and the tempo is 95 bpm. If that's too fast for you, deactivate the Master button on the Transport panel and slow the tempo before you record.

Figure P3.1 and 3.2 Jazz Funk score, pages
1 and 2.

Page 3

Page 4

Figure P3.3 and 3.4 Jazz Funk score, pages 3 and 4.

From the project 3 folder, load 3mix.cpr – the finished thing and have a good listen. Play it several times and follow the score. Sounds easier than it looks, doesn't it? Mute and solo tracks to hear individual tracks and sequences. The 'groove' is important here, and it is probably best to start this one with drums and bass.

Take 1

Track 7: Kick/Snare dr.
Quantize Selector: 1/8 Note.
Inspector: [out: lm-7] [chn: 10] [prg: Compressor] [map: GM map].
Transport panel: locators (l) 1.01.01 (R) 5.01.01 Activate AQ.

Follow these steps:

Figure P3.5 Kick and snare drums.

Figure P3.6 Kick and snare drums, Key Editor view.

1 Record (or enter manually in the Drum Editor) four bars of kick (C1) and snare (D1 or E1) drums (Figure P3.5, P3.6 and P3.7). Ensure that AQ (Automatic Quantize) is activated on the Transport panel.

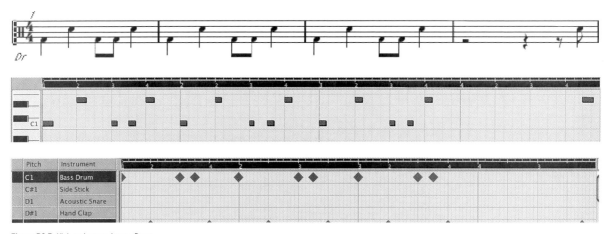

Figure P3.7 Kick and snare drums, Drum Editor view.

2 Select the newly recorded sequence and copy it to bar 5 [Edit > Repeat... x1] (Figure P3.8). That's eight bars of drums (1-9).
3 Save Project – compare with 3.1.cpr.

Figure 3.8 Repeat events.

Take 2

Track 6: Slap Bass.
Quantize Selector: 1/8 Note.
Inspector: [out: VB-1] [chn: 6] [prg: Slap Frets].Track Parameters: [Transpose: -12].
Transport panel: (L) 1.01.01. (R) 5.01.01. Activate AQ.

Info

Note the transposition of -12 in the Inspector for Track 6 (Track Parameters section). The reason for this? – bass guitar is written one octave higher than it actually sounds.

Follow these steps:

1 Record four bars of slap bass guitar (Figure P3.9 and 3.10).
2 Select the newly recorded part and copy it to bar 5.
3 Save Project – compare with 3.2.cpr.

Figure P3.9 Slap bass guitar.

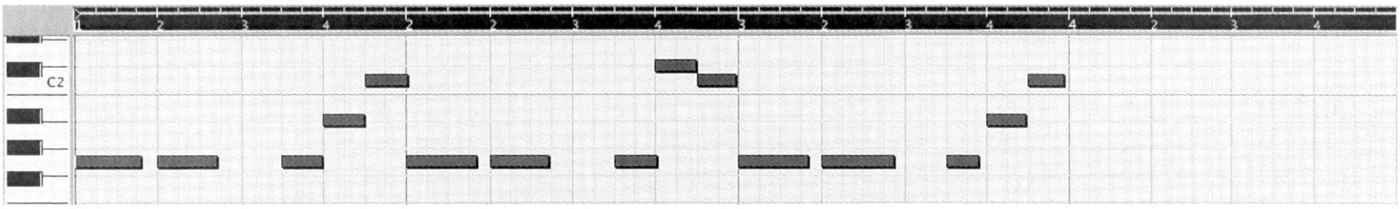

That's a basic drum and bass pattern established. Now for the horns. Trumpet first.

Figure P3.7 Slap bass guitar, Key Editor view.

Take 3

Track 1: Trumpet
Quantize Selector: 1/16 Note
Inspector: [out: GM] [chn: 1] [prg: 57]
Transport panel: (L) 1.01.01. (R) 5.01.01. Activate AQ.

Follow these steps:

1 Change the Quantize setting to 1/16 Note and record the trumpet between the locators, bars 1-5. Note bar 4 is blank (Figure P3.11 and 3.12).
2 Copy the new part to bar 5.

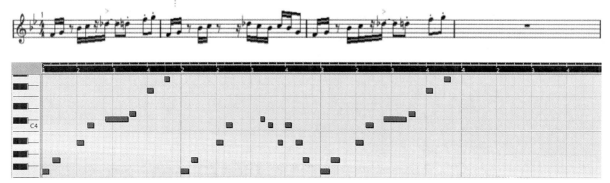

Figure P3.11 (top) Trumpet.

Figure P3.12 Trumpet, Key Editor view

3 Open the Key Editor, and from there open the Quantize Set-up box [MIDI > Quantize Set-up...] (Figure P3.13).

4 To inject some swing into that trumpet player, check the Auto box and experiment with the Swing slider. I have chosen 55% Swing as my quantize value (Figure P3.13). You may prefer another setting but anything much beyond that becomes too 'swingy' for the funk background. Once you have found a swing value you are happy with, use the Store button to save it as a pre-set for further use.

5 Save Project – compare with 3.3.cpr.

Figure 3.13 Quantize Set-up.

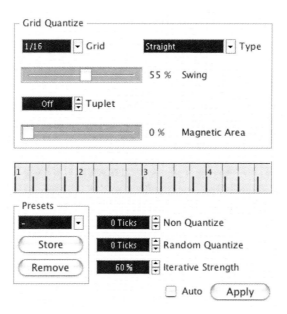

Tip

The Quantize Set-up dialogue box can be left open as you tweak the quantize settings in your projects. In fact, if you check the Auto box (bottom right hand corner) any changes made can be heard immediately. Very useful.

Figure P3.14 shows bars 1 – 5 of the non-quantised trumpet part displayed in the List Edit window. Compare these positions after 55% Swing has been applied (Figure P3.15).

You may be wondering why you are not using Iterative Quantize. There's so much of it in project 2 after all! Well hang on a bit. You'll humanise things a different way at the end of this project. Cubase SX/SL is a very flexible program and there's usually more than one way of doing things.

L	Type	Start	End	Length	Data 1	Data 2	Channel
	Note	0001.01.01.014	0001.01.01.111	0.0.0.97	F3	107	1
♩	Note	0001.01.02.009	0001.01.03.002	0.0.0.113	G3	105	1
♩	Note	0001.02.01.002	0001.02.01.100	0.0.0.98	A#3	100	1
♩	Note	0001.02.02.005	0001.02.02.092	0.0.0.87	C4	102	1
♩	Note	0001.02.04.053	0001.03.03.010	0.0.2.77	C#4	113	1
♩	Note	0001.03.03.018	0001.03.03.108	0.0.0.90	D4	105	1
♩	Note	0001.04.01.012	0001.04.01.105	0.0.0.93	F4	107	1
♩	Note	0001.04.03.007	0001.04.03.081	0.0.0.74	G4	116	1
♩	Note	0002.01.01.009	0002.01.01.119	0.0.0.110	F3	102	1
♩	Note	0002.01.02.010	0002.01.02.098	0.0.0.88	G3	110	1
♩	Note	0002.01.04.119	0002.02.01.098	0.0.0.99	A#3	105	1
♩	Note	0002.02.02.017	0002.02.02.103	0.0.0.86	C4	110	1
♩	Note	0002.03.02.049	0002.03.02.102	0.0.0.53	C#4	102	1
♩	Note	0002.03.03.038	0002.03.03.104	0.0.0.66	C4	87	1
♩	Note	0002.03.04.057	0002.04.01.003	0.0.0.66	A#3	98	1
♩	Note	0002.04.01.033	0002.04.01.117	0.0.0.84	C4	100	1
♩	Note	0002.04.02.036	0002.04.03.007	0.0.0.91	A#3	102	1
♩	Note	0002.04.03.029	0002.04.03.109	0.0.0.80	G3	98	1
♩	Note	0003.01.01.027	0003.01.02.029	0.0.1.2	F3	107	1
♩	Note	0003.01.02.000	0003.01.03.000	0.0.1.0	G3	105	1
♩	Note	0003.01.04.101	0003.02.01.085	0.0.0.104	A#3	113	1
♩	Note	0003.02.01.110	0003.02.02.088	0.0.0.98	C4	105	1
♩	Note	0003.02.04.020	0003.03.02.087	0.0.2.67	C#4	116	1
♩	Note	0003.03.02.091	0003.03.03.065	0.0.0.94	D4	102	1
♩	Note	0003.03.04.089	0003.04.01.053	0.0.0.84	F4	113	1
♩	Note	0003.04.02.080	0003.04.03.048	0.0.0.88	G4	116	1

Figure 3.14 The trumpet before quantizing.

L	Type	Start	End	Length	Data 1	Data 2	Channel
	Note	0001.01.01.000	0001.01.01.097	0.0.0.97	F3	107	1
♩	Note	0001.01.02.022	0001.01.03.015	0.0.0.113	G3	105	1
♩	Note	0001.02.01.000	0001.02.01.098	0.0.0.98	A#3	100	1
♩	Note	0001.02.02.022	0001.02.02.109	0.0.0.87	C4	102	1
♩	Note	0001.02.04.022	0001.03.02.099	0.0.2.77	C#4	113	1
♩	Note	0001.03.03.000	0001.03.03.090	0.0.0.90	D4	105	1
♩	Note	0001.04.01.000	0001.04.01.093	0.0.0.93	F4	107	1
♩	Note	0001.04.03.000	0001.04.03.074	0.0.0.74	G4	116	1
♩	Note	0002.01.01.000	0002.01.01.111	0.0.0.111	F3	102	1
♩	Note	0002.01.02.022	0002.01.02.110	0.0.0.88	G3	110	1
♩	Note	0002.02.01.000	0002.02.01.100	0.0.0.100	A#3	105	1
♩	Note	0002.02.02.022	0002.02.02.108	0.0.0.86	C4	110	1
♩	Note	0002.03.02.022	0002.03.02.074	0.0.0.52	C#4	102	1
♩	Note	0002.03.03.000	0002.03.03.066	0.0.0.66	C4	87	1
♩	Note	0002.03.04.022	0002.03.04.089	0.0.0.67	A#3	98	1
♩	Note	0002.04.01.000	0002.04.01.084	0.0.0.84	C4	100	1
♩	Note	0002.04.02.022	0002.04.02.113	0.0.0.91	A#3	102	1
♩	Note	0002.04.03.000	0002.04.03.080	0.0.0.80	G3	98	1
♩	Note	0003.01.01.000	0003.01.02.002	0.0.1.2	F3	107	1
♩	Note	0003.01.02.022	0003.01.03.022	0.0.1.0	G3	105	1
♩	Note	0003.02.01.000	0003.02.01.104	0.0.0.104	A#3	113	1
♩	Note	0003.02.02.022	0003.02.03.000	0.0.0.98	C4	105	1
♩	Note	0003.02.04.022	0003.03.02.088	0.0.2.66	C#4	116	1
♩	Note	0003.03.03.000	0003.03.03.095	0.0.0.95	D4	102	1
♩	Note	0003.04.01.000	0003.04.01.085	0.0.0.85	F4	113	1
♩	Note	0003.04.03.000	0003.04.03.088	0.0.0.88	G4	116	1

Figure P3.15 The trumpet after 55% Swing quantizing.

Take 4

Track 2: Tenor Sax
Quantize Selector: 1/16 Sw-55%
Inspector: [out: GM] [chn: 2] [prg: 67]
Track Parameters: [Transpose: -12]
Transport panel: (L) 1.01.01. (R) 5.01.01. Activate AQ.

Follow these steps:

1 Record the tenor sax between the locators. Note, bar 4 is blank (Figure P3.16 and P3.17). Again I have chosen a 1/16 Sw-55% for a quantize vale. If you chose another for the trumpet, on take 3, choose it again here otherwise the horns may sound sloppy.

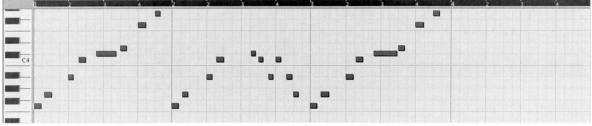

Figure P3.16 (top) Tenor sax.

Figure P3.17 Tenor sax., Key Editor view

2 Copy the new tenor sax sequence to bar 5.
3 Save Project – compare with 3.4.cpr.

Info

You may have noticed the figure eight just below the treble clef sign at the beginning of the tenor sax staff (P3.18). This tells us that the tenor sax is written one octave higher on the score than it actually sounds. That's why minus 12 has been entered in the Inspector Parameters for this take.

Figure P3.18 Treble clef with figure 8.

Take 5

Track 3: Trombone
Quantize Selector: 1/16 Sw-55%
Inspector: [out: GM] [chn: 3] [prg: 58]
Transport panel: (L) 1.01.01. (R) 5.01.01. Activate AQ.

Follow these steps:

1 Record the trombone part between the locators. (Figure P3.19 and P3.20).
2 Copy the new trombone sequence to bar 5.
3 Save Project – compare to 3.5.cpr.

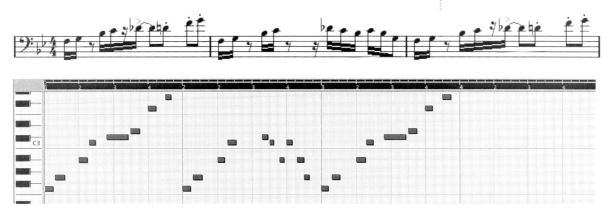

'Hang on a minute,' I hear you say, 'what about the notes in bar 4? They've been left out!' True, but that's a 'Solo Break' and you'll record it separately. All in good time!

Figure P3.19 (top) Trombone.

Figure P3.20 , Key Editor view

Take 6

Track 7: Kick/Snare dr.
Quantize Selector: 1/8 Note.
Transport panel: (L) 9.01.01 (R) 13.01.01. Activate AQ.

Follow these steps:

1 Change the Quantize setting to 1/8 Note and record, or enter in the Drum Editor, the drum pattern between the locators (Figure P3.21, P3.22 and P3.23).
2 Save Project – compare with 3.6.cpr.

Figure P3.21 Drums.

Figure P3.22 (below) Drums, Key Editor view.

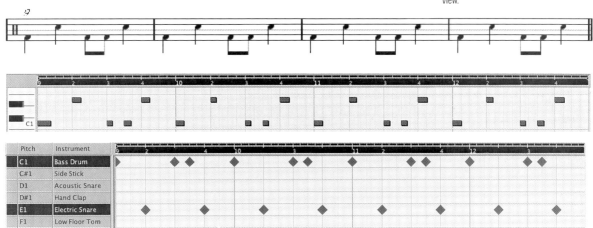

Figure P3.23 Drums, Drum Editor view.

Take 7

Track 6: Slap Bass.
Quantize Selector: 1/8 Note.
Transport panel: (L) 9.01.01 (R) 13.01 01. Activate AQ.

Follow these steps:

Figure P3.24 Slap bass.

1 Record the slap bass between the locators (Figure P3.24 and P3.25).
2 Save Project – compare with 3.7.cpr.

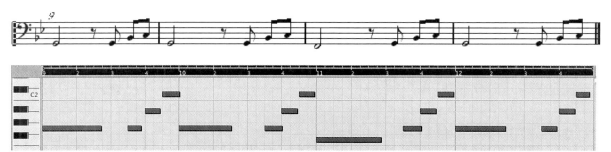

Figure P3.25 Slap bass, Key Editor view.

Take 8

Figure P3.26 Trumpet, tenor sax and trombone.

1 With the locators at (L) 9.01 01 (R) 13.01.01, record the trumpet, tenor and trombone on their respective tracks (Figure P3.26, P3.27). As before, be consistent with the quantizing. Mine is 1/16 Sw-55%.

Figure P3.27 (below) Trumpet, Key Editor view.

2 Save Project – compare with 3.8.cpr.

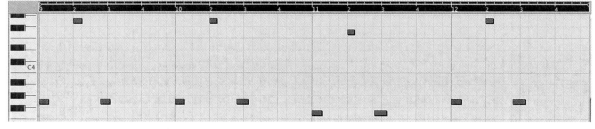

Take 9

1 With the locators at (L) 13.01 01 (R) 17.01 01, record the last four bars of
   drums and slap bass on their respective tracks (Figure P3.28, P3.29, P3.30
   and P3.31). Use 1/8 – Note quantizing.
2 Save Project.

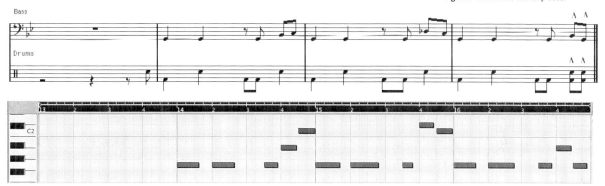

Figure P3.28 Drums and slap bass.

Figure P3.29 (above) Slap bass, Key Editor view.   **Figure P3.30 (below)** Drums, Key Editor view.

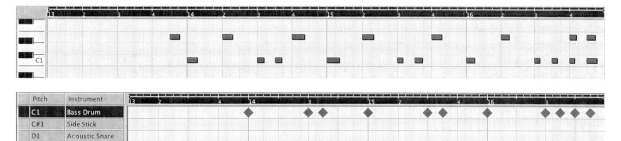

3 With the locators at (L) 14.01.01 (R) 17.01.01, record the last four bars of
   trumpet (no break in bar 13 just yet – be patient!), tenor sax and trombone on
   their respective tracks (Figure P3.32 and Figure P3.33). Again, be consistent
   with the quantize values (mine is 1/16Sw-55%).
4 Save Project – compare with 3.9.cpr.

Figure P3.31 Drums, Drum Editor view.

Figure P3.32 Trumpet, tenor sax and
trombone.

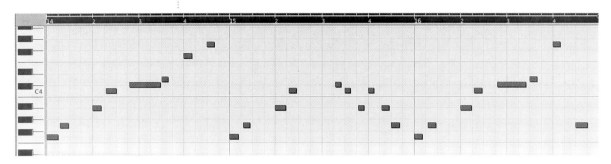

Figure P3.33 Trumpet, Key Editor view.

Take 10

Track 4: Dist. Gtr.
Quantize Selector: 1/16 Sw-55%.
Inspector: [out: GM] [chn: 4] [prg: 31]
Transport panel: (L) 1.1.1 (R) 5.1.1. Activate AQ.

Guitar parts are usually written one octave higher than they actually sound, even on a concert score. In this case, as you are probably playing a keyboard, it has been left at concert pitch. Play exactly as written, nice and choppy. Short notes. Follow these steps:

1 Record the guitar between the locators (Figure P3.34 and P3.35). If you have problems playing against the horn parts, mute them.

Figure P3.34 Distortion guitar.

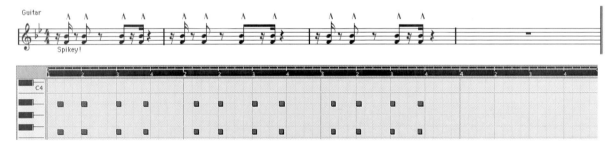

Figure P3.35 Distortion guitar, Key Editor view.

2 Copy the new part to bars 5 (5 – 8) and 14 (14 – 17).
3 Set the locators at (L) 9.01.01 (R) 13.01.01 and record the middle section (Figures P3.36 and P3.37).

Figure P3.36 More distortion guitar.

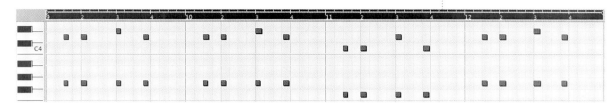

4 Save Project – compare with 3.10.cpr.

Figure P3.37 More distortion guitar, Key Editor view.

Take 11

Track 5: Rock Organ.
Quantize Selector: 1/8 Note.
Inspector: [out: GM] [chn: 5] [prg: 19].
Transport panel: (L) 1.01.01 (R) 5.01.01. Activate AQ.

Follow these steps:

1 Record the organ between the locators (Figure P3.38 and P3.39). Play it quietly, it's only a supporting part. Reducing the velocity value in the Inspector Parameter box will help achieve this.

Figure P3.38 Rock organ.

Figure P3.39 (below) Rock organ, Key Editor view.

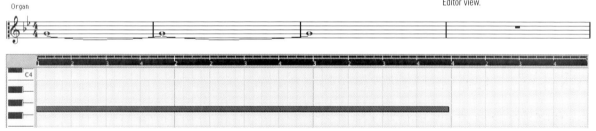

2 Copy the part to bars 5 (5 – 8) and 14 (14 – 17).
3 Change the locators to (L) 9.1.1 (R) 13.1 1 and record the middle section (Figure P3.40 and P3.41).
4 Save Project – compare with 3.11.cpr.

Figure P3.40 More rock organ.

Figure P3.41 (below) More rock organ, Key Editor view.

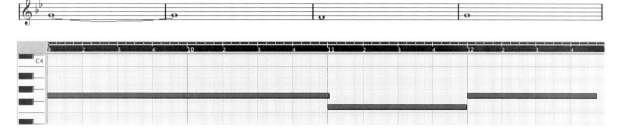

Tip

If you find it difficult to play with a light touch, reducing the velocity value in the Instrument Parameter box before you play will affect your performance in real time. Experiment with different values (Figure P3.42).

Figure P3.42 Reducing velocity.

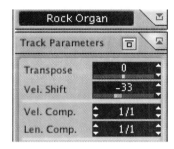

Take 12

Track 3: Trombone.
Transport panel: (L) 4.1.1 (R) 5.1.1.

OK, it's time to add those 'solo breaks.' You can copy the score or invent your own. You may have noticed that most of the parts are made up from the 'blues scale' beginning on G (G Bb C C# D F G). Try using it for your improvised breaks.

Follow these steps:

1. Ensure that AQ (Automatic Quantize) is turned off on the Transport panel. Leaving things without a quantize value this time will provide you with a more realistic performance.
2. Either record my trombone break (Figure P3.43 and P3.44), or better still, invent your own. Rule of thumb? – keep it simple!

Figure P3.43 Trombone break.

Figure P3.44 Trombone break, Key Editor view.

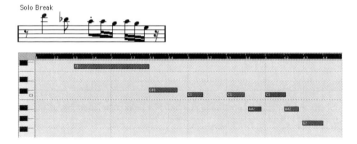

3 Record a tenor sax break (Figure P3.45 and P3.46).

Track: 2 Tenor Sax.
Transport Bar: (L) 8.1.1 (R) 9.1.1.

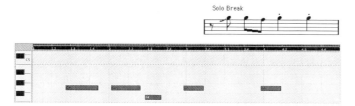

Figure P3.45 Tenor sax break.

Figure P3.46 Tenor sax break , Key Editor view.

4 Record a trumpet break (Figure P3.47 and P3.48).

Track 1: Trumpet.
Transport Bar: (L) 13.1 1 (R) 14.1 1.

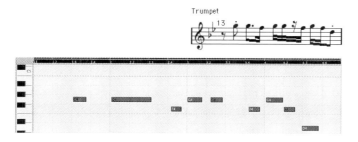

Figure P3.47 Trumpet break.

Figure P3.48 Trumpet break, Key Editor view.

Try adding some pitch bend data from your keyboard as you play the breaks. A trombonist will typically use his 'slide' for glissando effects in solos.

Figure 3.49 Pitch bend data, List Editor view, and
Figure 3.50 Key Editor view – the controller display.

Info

View the pitch bend data in the List Editor (Figure P3.49) or in the controller display, at the bottom of the Key Editor (Figure P3.50).

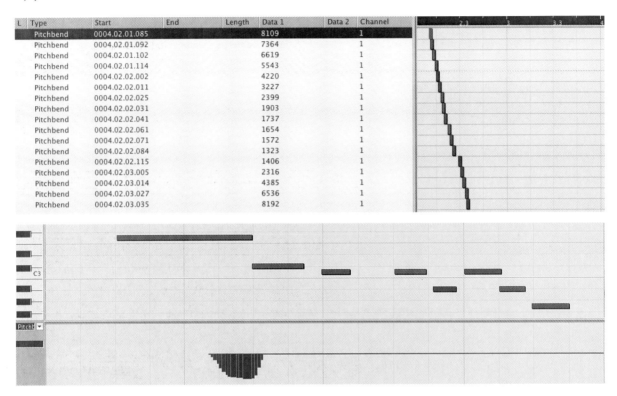

L	Type	Start	End	Length	Data 1	Data 2	Channel
	Pitchbend	0004.02.01.085			8109		1
	Pitchbend	0004.02.01.092			7364		1
	Pitchbend	0004.02.01.102			6619		1
	Pitchbend	0004.02.01.114			5543		1
	Pitchbend	0004.02.02.002			4220		1
	Pitchbend	0004.02.02.011			3227		1
	Pitchbend	0004.02.02.025			2399		1
	Pitchbend	0004.02.02.031			1903		1
	Pitchbend	0004.02.02.041			1737		1
	Pitchbend	0004.02.02.061			1654		1
	Pitchbend	0004.02.02.071			1572		1
	Pitchbend	0004.02.02.084			1323		1
	Pitchbend	0004.02.02.115			1406		1
	Pitchbend	0004.02.03.005			2316		1
	Pitchbend	0004.02.03.014			4385		1
	Pitchbend	0004.02.03.027			6536		1
	Pitchbend	0004.02.03.035			8192		1

5 Save Song – compare with 3.12.cpr.

Take 13

Track 8: Hi – Hat.
Quantize Selector: 1/16 Sw-55%.
Inspector: [out: lm-7] [chn: 10] [prg: Compressor] [map: GM Map].
Transport panel: (L) 9.1.1 (R) 13.1 1. Activate AQ.

Follow these steps:

1 Record the hi-hat between the locators (Figure P3.51, P3.52 and P3.53), closed (F#1).
2 Save Project – compare with 3.13.cpr.

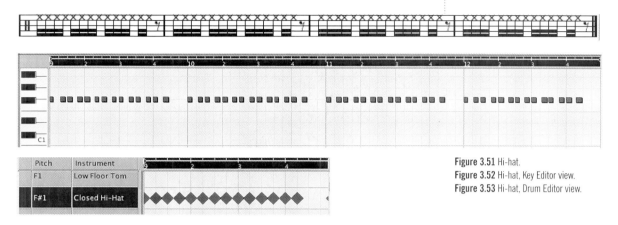

Figure **3.51** Hi-hat.
Figure **3.52** Hi-hat, Key Editor view.
Figure **3.53** Hi-hat, Drum Editor view.

Last, but not least, add the crash cymbal.

Take 14

Track 9: Crash Cymbal.
Quantize Selector: 1/8 – Note.
Inspector: [out: lm-7] [chn: 10] [prg: Compressor] [map: GM Map].
Transport Bar: (L) 9.1 1 (R) 13.1 1.

Follow these steps:

1 Record the cymbal crashes – C#2 (Figure P3.54 and P3.55).
2 Save Project – compare with 3.14.cpr.

Figure **3.54** Cymbal crashes.
Figure **3.55** Cymbal crashes, Drum Editor
view.

The mix

In Project 2 you changed the pan settings in the Inspector from the Project window. You can also control volume from there. However, there is a more intuitive method.

1 Open the Mixer [Devices > Mixer]. A virtual mixing console appears with a channel strip for each track used (Figure P3.56).

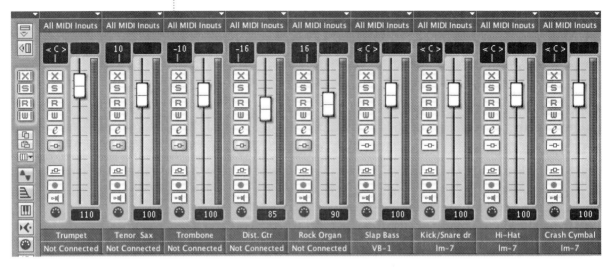

Figure 3.56 The Mixer.

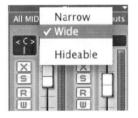

Figure 3.57 View Options .

Figure 3.58 View Options, Common panel strip.

2 Use the channel strip faders to balance volume and the pan control sliders – check 'Wide' in the View Options pop-up to see them – to create a stereo picture (Figure P3.57).

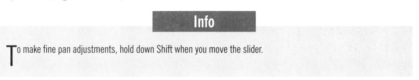

Info

To make fine pan adjustments, hold down Shift when you move the slider.

3 It would be nice to add a little reverberation to those General MIDI instruments, don't you think? Start with the trumpet on track 1. You'll need to see the Extended channel strip first so click the View Options in the Common panel strip – it's on the left – or click on the Extended/Normal Mixer icon (Figure P3.58a and P3.58b). Check 'Expanded' in the pop-up and the Extended channel strip (SX only) appears above the Normal channel strip (Figure P3.59).

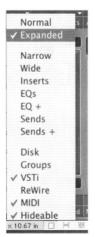

Figure 3.58a Extended/Normal Mixer icon.

4 You're going to add reverberation via a channel insert so click on the Show All Inserts icon – on the left (Fig P3.60).

Figure 3.60
Show All Inserts icon .

Figure 3.59 Extended mixer (SX only).

5 The reverberation on a GM sound module responds to controller number ninety-one. Using Insert 1, select 'Control'from the inserts pop-up menu (Figure P3.61). The Control panel appears. Using one of the eight controller boxes – on the right – select 'ExtEff 1 Depth'from the pop-up (This is actually controller ninety-one). Use the slider – on the left – to add a moderate amount of reverberation (Figure P3.62).

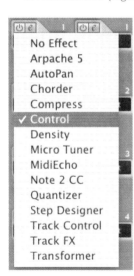

Figure 3.61 Inserts available.

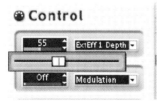

Figure 3.62 Control panel.

6 In the same way, add a little reverberation to the other GM instruments. The two VST Instruments, drums, lm-7 and bass, VB-1 can be left untreated for now. See project 5 for adding effects to VST Instruments.

Tip

For those of you who have not used reverberation before, beware! – use sparingly. Too much will muddy the mix.

Settings made in the Mixer are reflected in the Inspector. For example the inserted controller ninety-one (reverberation) can be seen in the Inserts folder (Figure P3.63). For many users this presents a clearer less cluttered alternative to using the mixer.

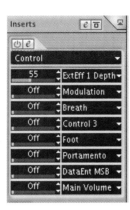

Figure 3.63 Inserts folder.

A finishing touch: the brass section sounds real tight! Too tight maybe. The answer? – humanise it.

1 Open the List Editor [MIDI > Open List Editor]. The sequence was quantized using a value of 1/16 Sw-55% and should look like figure P3.64 This is fine but all three horns are playing in unison, except for the middle section. Had they been in three part harmony things would be a little better but as it is, only their note lengths are different.

Figure 3.64 Trumpet quantized with 1/16 Sw-55%, List Editor view.

L	Type	Start	End	Length	Data 1
♩	Note	0001.01.01.000	0001.01.01.097	0.0.0.97	F3
♩	Note	0001.01.02.022	0001.01.03.015	0.0.0.113	G3
♩	Note	0001.02.01.000	0001.02.01.098	0.0.0.98	A#3
♩	Note	0001.02.02.022	0001.02.02.109	0.0.0.87	C4
♩	Note	0001.02.04.022	0001.03.02.099	0.0.2.77	C#4
♩	Note	0001.03.03.000	0001.03.03.090	0.0.0.90	D4
♩	Note	0001.04.01.000	0001.04.01.093	0.0.0.93	F4
♩	Note	0001.04.03.000	0001.04.03.074	0.0.0.74	G4
♩	Note	0002.01.01.000	0002.01.01.111	0.0.0.111	F3
♩	Note	0002.01.02.022	0002.01.02.110	0.0.0.88	G3
♩	Note	0002.02.01.000	0002.02.01.100	0.0.0.100	A#3
♩	Note	0002.02.02.022	0002.02.02.108	0.0.0.86	C4

2 Return to the Project window, select track 1 (trumpet) and in the Inspector, select the Track Parameters.

3 Using the pop-ups in the Random settings, change 'OFF' to 'Position' and set minimum and maximum randomise positions of -5 and 5 (Figure P3.65). You can, off course, enter higher values but too much will destroy the swing feel set up earlier in the project.

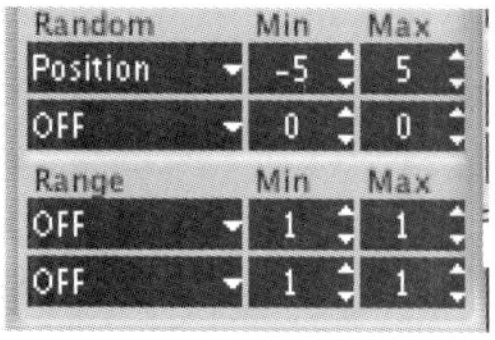

Figure 3,65 Random settings.

Info

Randomisation of note position is possibly the most useful of the Random settings and can be set between -500 to +500 ticks. Pitch, Velocity and Length can also be randomised.

Tip

After randomisation, on the processed tracks, it's quite likely that the very first notes in bar 1 will be pushed just ahead of the beat. Change them back to 1.01.01. or you will not hear them!

6 Repeat this operation on the tenor sax and trombone tracks. The result will still be very tight but just that little bit more realistic sounding.

The process can also be applied to the rhythm section. I've used a randomise value of -10 and +10 on the slap bass. Go too far though and the band will sound like they've been at the bar too long before the gig!

7 Save Project – compare with 3mix.cpr.

Project 4: a classical score

Musical objectives

- Sequence a short extract from Mozart's Clarinet Concerto.
- Achieve a convincing interpretation of a string orchestra and solo clarinet.
- Position the instruments in a realistic stereo picture.

Cubase SX/SL skills

- Using Transpose in the Track Parameters.
- Applying compression using the MIDI plug-in named Compress as an Insert effect.
- Applying Legato to slurred notes using either the Key or Score Editors.
- Automating the Mixer.

Preparation

1 From the CD, copy the folder named 'project 4' to your desktop.
2 Inside the 'project 4' folder you'll find a file named 'template4.cpr.' Open it and use it for this project.
3 Create a folder in which to save your own files as you work through the project.

OK this is Mozart. Don't be scared. It's not difficult. It's slow for a start! To begin with, load automix.cpr from the project 4 folder and have a listen as you view the score. Play it through several times until it becomes familiar.

The clarinet solo is in from bar 1, so get that down first and take it from there.

Take 1

Track 1: Clarinet.
Quantize Selector: 1/8 Note.
Inspector: [out: GM] [chn: 1] [prg 72].
Track Parameters: [Transpose -2].
Transport panel: (L) 1.01.01 (R) 5.01.01. Activate AQ.

Take a look at the score (Figures P4.1, P4.2, P4.3 and P4.4).   65

Clarinet Concerto

Mozart

Figure P4.1 and 4.2 Clarinet concerto score, pages 1 and 2.

The strings are written in Eb (three flats) and the clarinet in F (one flat). This is because clarinets are pitched in Bb. When Bb is played on the piano a clarinet plays the note C. Without getting into the complexities of a thorough explanation, what this means is you read and play the score as written and transpose it down a tone. To achieve this it is necessary to enter -2 in the Sequence Parameters box.

Page 3

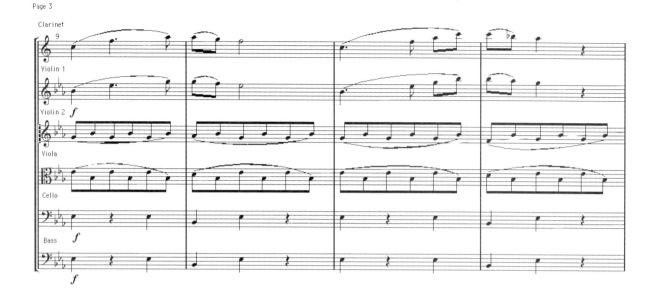

Page 4

In order to achieve a nice smooth classical clarinet sound you may well need to apply some compression (Figure P4.5). I used a compression factor of 1/2 and a velocity shift of 33. Your settings will depend on your playing style. Page 427 in the Cubase SX/SL operation manual explains all.

Figure P4.3 and 4.4 Clarinet concerto score, pages 3 and 4.

Compress is a very useful MIDI compressor plug-in used for smoothing out or expanding differences in velocity. It's interface emulates a standard audio compressor. Only notes above the Threshold parameter are affected. The Ratio parameter determines the rate of compression applied to those velocities. The Gain parameter adds or subtracts a fixed value from the velocities.

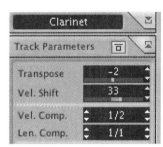

Figure P4.5 Applying compression.

Follow these steps:

1 Record the first four bars of clarinet (Figure P4.6 and P4.7). Play in a nice legato style. Any overlapping notes can be cleaned up afterwards.

Figure P4.6 Clarinet.

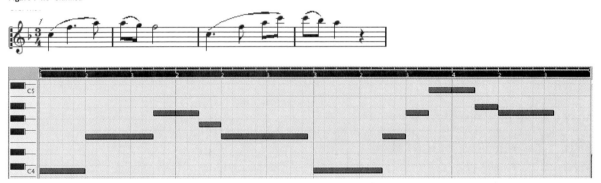

Figure P4.7 Clarinet, Key Editor view

Tip

If you don't want to be bothered with gluing parts together, on the Transport panel, set Rec Mode to Merge. Leaving it set to Normal will give separate parts for separate takes.

Tip

Always leave the last note under a slur deselected before applying Legato. Think about it!

2 On the Toolbar, change the quantize value to 1/16 Note. This is to take account of the sixteenth note in bar 8. Set the locators to cycle between 5.01.01 and 9.01.01 and record the next four bars (Figure P4.8 and P4.9). Glue the two resulting sequences together to make a part eight bars long.

3 Listen back. I mentioned earlier about woodwind players articulating with their tongues. Where a slur joins a group of notes only the first note is slurred. Some editing is necessary to achieve this effect.

4 From within either the Score or Key Editor windows, select all the notes under each slur, except the last, and apply Legato [MIDI > Functions > Legato]

5 The following eight bars are an exact repetition of the first so copy the new sequence (bars 1–9) to bar 9. You now have sixteen bars. Clean up any overlapping notes – impossible on a clarinet – by viewing the parts in the Key Edit window, selecting all the events, and applying [MIDI > Functions > Delete Overlaps (poly/mono).

6 Save Project – compare with 4.1.cpr.

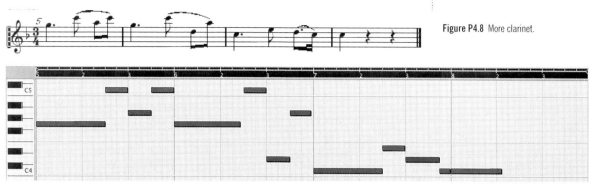

Figure P4.8 More clarinet.

Figure P4.9 More clarinet, Key Editor view.

Take 2

Track 2: Violin 1.
Quantize Selector: 1/8 Note.
Inspector: [out: GM] [chn: 2] [prg 49].
Transport panel: (L) 1.01.01 (R) 9.01.01. Activate AQ.

You are simulating a small string orchestra here so use Program 49 – Strings – and not an individual instrument. You can of course use single instruments if you wish, but the effect will be somewhat thinner. The nature of this concerto, I think, benefits from a rather more lush background.

Follow these steps:

1 Record the first eight bars of the violin 1 part (Figure P4.10 and P4.11). Break it down into smaller sections if necessary. Adjust the compression to suit your playing style.
2 Listen back, and as with the clarinet part, apply Legato to the slurred notes and clean up any audible overlaps with the Note Overlap Correction functions. Small overlaps on legato strings often work and can be left alone if they sound nice.
3 Save Project – compare with 4.2.cpr.

Figure P4.10 Violin 1.

Figure P4.11 Violin 1, Key Editor view.

Take 3

Track 3: Violin 2.
Quantize Selector: 1/8 Note.
Inspector: [out: GM] [chn: 3] [prg 49].
Transport panel: (L) 1.01.01 (R) 9.01.01. Activate AQ.

Follow these steps:

1 Record the first eight bars of violin 2 (Figure P4.12 and P4.13). Apply Legato and clean up as in Take 2.
2 Save Project – compare with 4.3.cpr.

Figure P4.12 Violin 2.

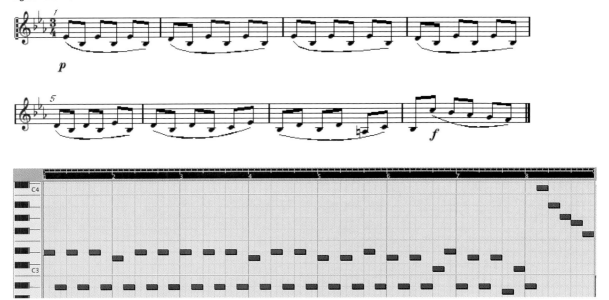

Figure P4.13 Violin 2, Key Editor view.

Take 4

Track 4: Viola
Quantize Selector: 1/8 Note.
Inspector: [out: GM] [chn: 4] [prg 49].
Transport panel: (L) 1.01.01 (R) 9.01.01. Activate AQ.

Follow these steps:

1 Record the first eight bars of Viola (Figure P4.14 and P4.15). Viola parts are written in alto clef. Middle C is on the middle line of the staff. As with the violins, apply Legato and clean up where necessary.
2 Save Project – compare with 4.4.cpr.

Tip

An easy way to read and play from the alto clef: in the Instrument Parameter box, enter a Transpose value of -10 and play the part as if reading from the treble clef.

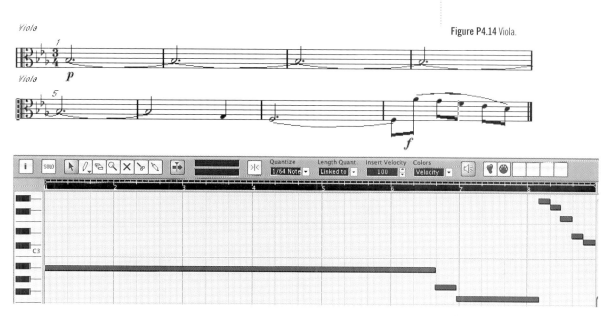

Figure P4.14 Viola.

Figure P4.15 Viola, Key Editor view.

Take 5

Track 5: Cello
Quantize Selector: 1/8 Note.
Inspector: [out: GM] [chn: 5] [prg 49].
Inserts: Compress: [Threshold 80] [Ratio 2:1] [Gain 0]
Transport panel: (L) 1.01.01 (R) 9.01.01. Activate AQ.

Follow these steps:

1 Record the first eight bars of cello (Figure P4.16 and P4.17). If you play it carefully, Legato need not be applied. However, you may have to use the Note Overlap Correction functions. I did!
2 Save Project – compare with 4.5.cpr.

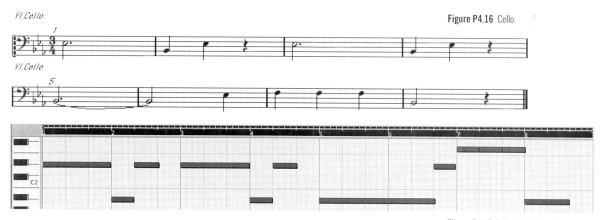

Figure P4.16 Cello.

Figure P4.17 Cello, Key Editor view.

Take 6

Quantize Selector: 1/16 Note.
Inspector: [out: GM] [chn: 2] [prg 49].
Transport panel: (L) 9.01.01 (R) 17.01.01. Activate AQ.

Follow these steps:

1   Record the remaining eight bars of violin 1 (Figure P4.18 and P4.19). (Note: Quantize Value is now 1/16 – Note) Break it down into four bar sections if you wish. Apply Legato and clean up note lengths.

Figure P4.18 Violin 1.

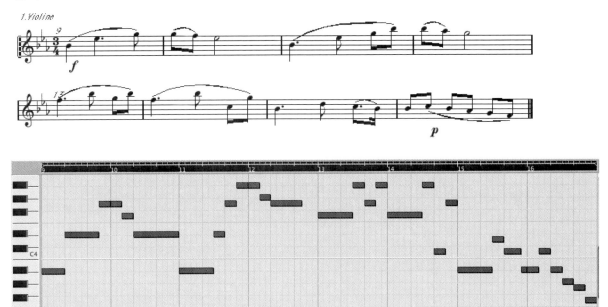

Figure P4.19 Violin 1, Key Editor view.

Take a look at the score again. Bars 9 – 17 of violin 2 are almost the same as bars 1 – 9 of violin 1. No point in making extra work!

2   Select the violin 1 sequence (bars 1 – 9) and drag a copy over to bar 9 on track 3 (violin 2).

3   There are of course five notes to add to this new part in bar 16 (Figures P4.20 and P4.21). Return to track 3 (violin 2), set the locators at (L) 16.01.01 (R) 17.01.01 and overdub them. Apply Legato and clean up any overlapped notes.

Figure P4.20 Violin 2, five more notes.

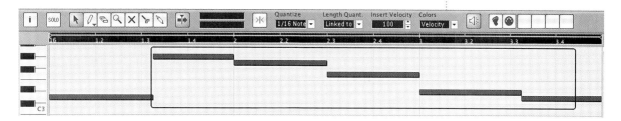

4 To avoid confusion, it's a good idea to glue the new violin 2 parts (9 – 17) together and rename the resulting single part 'Violin 2'. This can be done in the Project Browser. Note the colour changes automatically.

Figure P4.21 Violin 2, five more notes, Key Editor view.

Info

It's often a good idea to organise tracks and sequences by colour. Select a track or object and use the colour palette on the Toolbar to select your favourite colours (Figure P4.22).

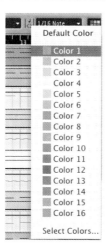

Figure P4.22 Selecting colours.

Another glance at the score also tells us that the viola part between bars 9 and 17 is also a duplication of the violin 2 part between bars 1 and 9.

5 Select the violin 2 sequence (bars 1 – 9) and drag a copy over to bar 9 on track 4 (viola).

6 This time there are five notes to delete in bar 16 (Figure P4.23). Selecting them in either the Key or Score Editors and pressing the delete key on your computer keyboard is probably the easiest method of doing this. You may well need to lengthen the remaining note in this bar. Selecting it in the Key Editor window and resizing it is probably the simplest way of doing this.

7 Again, it's a good idea to rename the sequence 'Viola'.

8 Save Project – compare with 4.6.cpr

Delete these notes

Figure P4.23

Take 7

> *Track 5:* Cello.
> *Quantize Selector:* 1/8 Note.
> *Inspector:* [out: GM] [chn: 5] [prg 49].
> *Transport panel:* (L) 9.01.01 (R) 17.01.01. Activate AQ.

Follow these steps:

1 Record the cello between the locators (Figure 4.24 and P4.25). Clean up.
2 Save Project – compare with 4.7.cpr.

Figure P4.24 Cello.

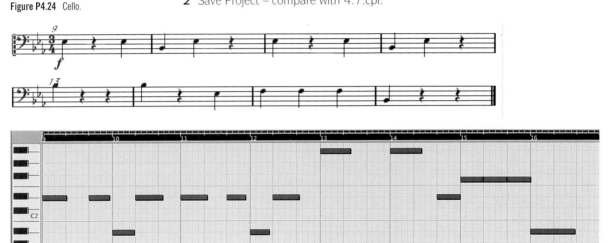

Figure P4.25 Cello, Key Editor view.

Take 8

> *Track 6:* Double Bass
> *Quantize Selector:* 1/8 Note.
> *Inspector:* [out: GM] [chn: 1] [prg 49].
> *Transport panel:* (L) 9.01.01 (R) 17.01.01. Activate AQ.

Have a look at the double bass part on the score. You have probably noticed that it looks identical to the cello part above it. Well it is, but with one exception. The double bass sounds an octave lower than it is written. You now have a choice – either record the bass part in the usual way or copy the cello sequence to track 7 and transpose it down one octave.

Although it takes a little longer, I prefer the first option. Why? Because the velocities and note lengths will be different and this adds to the overall realism of the sequence. Two sequences with identical data, playing together, often sounds naff!

Follow these steps:

1 Record the double bass between the locators (Figure P4.26 and P4.27).
Ensure that transposition is set to -12 in the Track Parameters. Clean up any
overlaps.
2 Save Project – compare with 4.8.cpr.

Figure P4.26 Double bass.

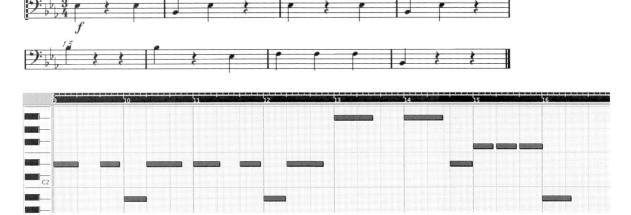

Figure P4.27 Double bass, Key Editor view.

Automated mix

1 Open the Mixer [Devices > Mixer]. A mixer appears containing six channel
strips that correspond to our six tracks in the Project window. The track names
are listed at the bottom of each strip. The faders are for controlling volume.
2 Play the piece through and adjust the volume levels until you achieve an
acceptable balance. Now this is a clarinet solo, so obviously that instrument
needs to be louder than the others. Note: on the score, the first eight measures
of the strings are marked piano (quiet). My levels were set as follows:

Figure 4.28 Volume and Pan mix.

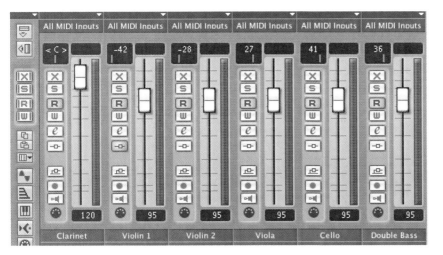

> **Tip**
>
> When mixing, keep the solo
> instrument – in this case the
> clarinet – in the centre of the stereo
> picture and, if necessary, raise its
> volume for prominence.

In a real string orchestra 1st and 2nd violins are positioned to the left of the conductor and the viola and cellos to the right. The double basses are behind the violas and cellos. To achieve something similar in our stereo picture:

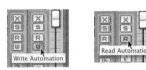
3 Adjust the pan control – the sliders to the left of the faders – Wide view (Figure P4.28) – to the following:

Clarinet: 0 in the centre. It's his/her big moment!
Violin 1: minus 42
Violin 2: minus 28
Viola: 27
Cello: 41
Double Bass: 36

4 Return to the Project window. You will notice that the volume and pan settings in the Inspector have changed to reflect the mixer settings.
5 Refer to the score. In bar 8 (at 8.01.03. to be precise) the strings change to forte (loud). Set up a cycle starting a bar or two before the forte mark – *f* – and ending a bar or so afterwards.
6 Return to the Mixer, and cycle the music whilst you practise raising the fader levels for the strings to about 105 each time the music reaches bar 8.
7 When you're ready activate the Write button on the Common Panel strip (Figure P4.29), and channel by channel, record the fader movements. The data will be recorded into their respective tracks. When you're finished turn off the Write button.
8 Activate the Read button on the Common Channel strip (Figure P4.30) and play the sequence back. Gaze in wonder as the faders move all by themselves when the music reaches bar 8! I love it. Could watch them all day. Sad, really, isn't it?
9 Save Project – compare with 4automix.cpr.

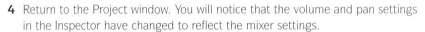

Figures 4.29 and 4.30 Automation – Write and Read buttons

Figure 4.31 You can view the automation data in the Project window using Edit > Show Used Automation.

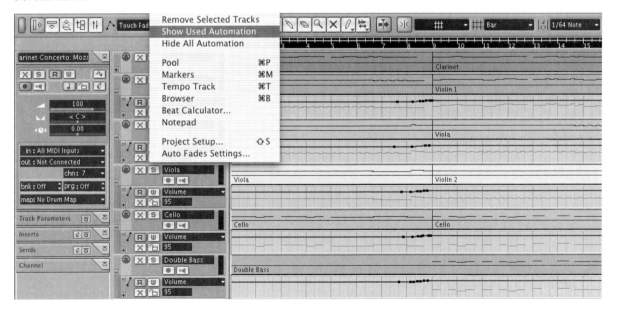

One more thing. Open the Mixer and you'll notice that reverberation has been used as an Insert on all channels. This will address your GM sound module. Read the mix instructions in project 3 for instructions on how to do this.

The HALion String Edition Mix

General MIDI sound modules and soft synths often do a pretty good job of emulating a string orchestra but they will not fool a trained ear. To get results close to the real thing you need a good orchestral sample library. There's only one drawback, these can cost a small fortune. However, all is not lost. Steinberg produce a VST Instrument called the HALion String Edition (Figure P4.32). It comes complete with a set of first class string samples, suitable for general use, integrates perfectly with Cubase SX/SL and will not break the bank.

Figure 4.32 HALion String Edition.

Open 4halion.cpr to hear an alternative mix (Figure P4.33).

* The clarinet part was re-recorded as an audio track using a Proteus/2 Orchestral sound module. This was an act of extreme laziness because I could have played it myself! The original MIDI track (muted) has been retained. Note the volume changes in the automation track. These help to make it more realistic. Note too, how the clarinet track has been delayed, just a little. This is enough to set it apart from the violins which play in unison from bar 9. EQ has been used to cut the lower mid frequencies (Figure P3.34).

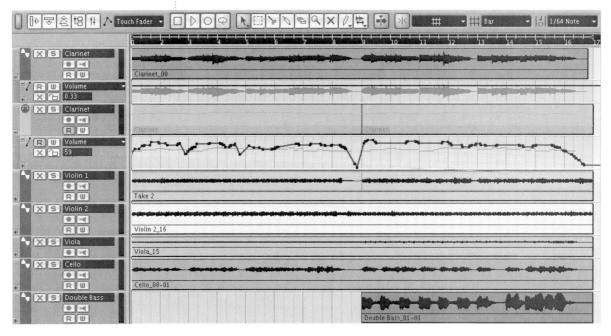

Figure 4.33 4halionmix.cpr

- The HALion String Edition's violins and violas were not treated with EQ (you are welcome to experiment) but the celli and basses were given a boost at the bottom end (Figures P4.35 and P3.36).

Clarinet

Cello

Double Bass

Figure 4.34 (left) EQ, clarinet lower mid frequencies cut.
Figure 4.34 (mid) EQ, celli lower frequency boost.
Figure 4.34 (right) EQ, basses lower frequency boost.

All tracks were treated with a little reverb supplied by the Reverb A plug-in, used as a send effect.

Finding and developing ideas

So far I have talked about and sequenced other people's music – well mine actually, apart from the classical stuff – and I'm sure you are itching to put some of the topics covered into practice by composing music of your own. Before you can start doing this you will need ideas. No doubt some of you will have dozens of ideas already. Many people though, find it difficult to be inventive and will either stare blankly at the screen or doodle for hours with nothing to show for it at the end. 'I can't think of anything', they say.

The old saying, 'Composing is one percent inspiration and ninety-nine percent hard work', is spot on. Beethoven for example – a creative genius if ever there was one – would tortuously rework a fragment of melody over and over until he considered it perfect. From that one tiny idea a symphony would develop. One percent eureka, ninety-nine percent hard graft. So it is for the rest of us in most cases.

Finding new ideas

So how do we get ideas for compositions in the first place? Can we use Cubase SX/SL? Will Cubase give us ideas? Well it might. It's not my favourite way to start but it undoubtedly works for some. If you are constructing loop based techno or dance music then using sample CDs with pre-recorded material is the obvious way to go. However, this will not work very well if you've been given a specific brief for a commercial project and you are being paid for it. Other people's licks are not guaranteed to fit the bill. Even if the style of music requires loops and grooves it may well be quicker to invent and record your own. The result is going to be far more original for a start.

At the computer?

A tentative yes. Keep control. A computer running Cubase SX/SL is a very powerful tool, and a tool is all that it is. It will not, as some mistakenly believe, compose or arrange your music for you. Does a carpenter tell his tools to build him a beautiful piece of furniture, sit back, open a six pack and watch? He'd have a long wait.

There are special random generator programs available which will turn small ideas into complete compositions of a sort. These are great for experimental music, but I'm sure even the authors of such software would be the first to admit that they are not intended for producing commercial music.

You could import MIDI files into Cubase SX/SL, chop up the material and reuse it for your own compositions. Not really a good idea though. You could end up in court for breach of copyright!

What about importing classical music MIDI files, chopping those up and reworking them? After all the composers are mostly long dead and the tunes are out of copyright. Well you can I suppose, in fact I can think of one well known composer who does just that or something similar – but it will not help much if you've been asked to supply background music for a motor racing video clip!

No, I'm sorry, ideas are what we need and where is the best place to get them?

Away from the computer?

Leonard Bernstein got them lying on the sofa and staring at the ceiling. When his wife entered the room and asked him what he was doing, he would reply, 'I'm working!'

One thing's for sure. Ideas come more readily if you tell your subconscious that you want them. You may think this is barmy but it works. Give your subconscious instructions. Be specific and set a deadline. Start small. Don't ask for a symphony. You will not get it! Something like: 'I want the beginnings of a tune for a children's song by tomorrow morning'. The more you develop this habit of asking for ideas the more they begin to come. It's habit forming and self generating. Ideas generate more ideas.

I get ideas first thing in the morning as soon as I wake up. They are usually melodic – I don't dream chord sequences – and fortunately my bedroom is right next door to my studio, so I can leap (crawl, more like) out of bed, boot up Cubase SX/SL and record them before breakfast. After the all important pot of tea, I can evaluate these gems, delete them (often the case) or file them away in an ideas folder for later development.

Ideas tend to come in a flash and often fade away just as quick. It's important to act quickly and retain them somehow. If you have a great memory, then fine. If not and you are familiar with music notation then it's a simple matter of keeping a manuscript note pad handy. A portable mini disk recorder and vocal chords are an alternative.

Don't doodle!

'What a load of rubbish! ' I hear you say. 'I get my ideas at the keyboard. I fire up Cubase, press Record and improvise until the ideas start to flow'. Surely that's the best way to get ideas.

Well good on you. That's great. I envy you. Trouble is, I can't do that, and nor can many others.

For those of you who are good keyboard payers I have only one word of warning. Beware of doodling. Improvising is not composition. Well it is, in a group environment when we tear off a solo on our chosen instrument over a predetermined chord sequence. For this we generally need a good technique. There lies the problem.

A common scenario. A keyboard player with a fantastic technique sits down at his synthesiser to compose and record in Cubase SX/SL. What happens? Before he knows it his fingers have taken over. They are following patterns that have been learned and subconsciously stored over the years. Out they all come and into

Cubase SX/SL they all go. A half hour later he plays it all back. Has he got a composition at the end of it? I doubt it. Music composed or arranged for a specific purpose generally needs discipline and a degree of planning. A balanced composition, particularly a lengthy one, is rarely conceived as an improvisation. That half hour may have been better spent lying on his back like Leonard Bernstein.

Developing your ideas

Dave's got a great idea for a tune. It came like a bolt of lightning while he was waiting for the bus. He hums all the way home – in case he forgets it – and quickly records the melody into Cubase as an eight bar lead synth part. 'It's brilliant', he thinks. 'Absolutely brilliant!' He cycles it round a few times and hits upon a killer bass line. 'Fantastic!', he yells.' He improvises some drums over that and records a funky chord sequence using a favourite guitar patch. 'This is it. This is gonna make me a fortune', he cries. 'Strings! It needs strings', he bellows, and he sets about adding a string pad. Already his musical canvas is pretty full. He can't think of anything else to add at the moment so he saves the file and goes off to make a cup of tea.

A while later Dave returns to his masterpiece. He plays the eight bars. 'Hmm, it's only eight bars long. It definitely needs more, but I can't think of anything else. I know, I'll do a rough mix instead. Something will come to me later.'

Dave sets about the mix and experiments with the levels in the Cubase mixer. He used the A1 VST Instrument for the lead synth so he opens up his VST send effects rack and adds some chorus and reverb effects (does it really need them, I wonder?). A couple of hours later he sits back to have a listen. 'Mmm, it doesn't sound quite as good now. It's not quite what I had in mind when I was on the bus. Perhaps that bass line needs to be a bit different. ' And so he changes the bass line, which in turn requires a modification to the chord sequence. 'That's better, but hold on, the melody needs altering to fit that new chord.' Dave alters the melody. Oh dear! Wasn't that the brilliant bit, conceived at the bus stop. 'I'm not sure about that kick drum, it doesn't sound fat enough. Where's that article I read in *Sound on Sound*, about compression, it's here somewhere. Oh well, maybe some EQ instead.'

He's lost the plot now, although I'm not so sure he had one in the first place. It all started so promising as well. What did he do wrong? Well he didn't know where he was going for a start.

Know where you are heading

Those sudden flashes of inspiration, so often likened to thunderbolts, the eureka if you like, are wonderful. Trouble is, once recorded they often turn into short, rather stubborn, fragments of material that refuse to move on. Why? Probably because we have not decided what we want to do in the first place.

The mind works all the time in the background. It will throw up all kinds of great, but totally unrelated ideas. If we decide what we want to write first, and then instruct our subconscious mind to get on with it, we stand a much better chance.

If someone has been commissioned to compose or arrange a piece of music for a specific purpose it is much easier to get going. The plan has been provided, and if you expect to be paid, then you had better stick pretty close to it. If however you want to write for the sheer pleasure of it of it, maybe for practice, then it's a good idea to invent a brief of your own. Give yourself a purpose for writing. Here's a rough guide on how to set about it.

1 Decide exactly what it is you want to write and why. If you are not sure, invent something like 'a local sports shop needs a short radio jingle'. Have a specific business in mind. You never know, if it turns out well they may decide to invest in a radio advertisement on the strength of your idea.

2 Decide what style the music should take and what instruments or sounds you intend to use. Obviously things may change, but it helps to have a clear mental picture from the outset as to how things will sound.

3 Decide on a basic form. If you can't envisage one mentally, invent one on paper. Keep it simple. ABA maybe. At least that way you have a structure to hang things on.

Now you know where you are heading. You have defined a set of problems to solve with your own skill and musical craftsmanship. Even if the result doesn't quite make it, you can get started and modify it later. As I said earlier, the mind is working constantly, all the time, in the background. If Dave had followed this route after that initial eureka he would maybe have recorded the broad outline of his project, and having done so had a further brilliant idea to help fill in the details, perhaps whilst waiting for the bus the next day. That's another thing the mind tends to do. Through up ideas at certain times and places.

Keep moving – work creates work

It is most important to keep moving. It can be a very daunting experience to stare at a blank Arrange window in Cubase and not be able to start. Once you have set your criteria record anything that it suggests. If you can only think up a tiny fragment of a tune, don't worry. Record it. That's enough. Beethoven built huge musical masterpieces from just such fragments. Don't dwell on it, but move on. Does that first phrase suggest something else? Does it beg an answer? Can it be repeated? Upside down or back to front. Keep moving. The more you write, even if it is not very good, the easier it will become. Work creates work and ideas produce yet more ideas. You can refine and improve them later.

Repetition and variation

OK so how do we keep things flowing if we can't think of anything? One method of course is simple repetition. It's an essential ingredient of most music. So many beginners are scared stiff to repeat an idea, afraid that it will be boring to do so. On the contrary, an opening phrase will often set an air of expectancy. When this phrase is repeated, the listener's subconscious picks up on it and a basic psychological and emotional sense of musical fulfilment is achieved. Of course it would be utterly boring if the same phrase were repeated endlessly. This is why we also need variation. Repetition and variation, hand in hand. Together they make a very powerful composition tool for almost any style of music.

Keep it simple – details later

As well as moving on it is important to keep it simple. Save the detail until later. If it's melodic material the details such as choice of harmony and rhythm will suggest themselves at a later stage. This is exactly what Dave did not do. He started right. He recorded eight bars of terrific melody, but then stopped and concentrated on the detail instead of moving forward. Paralysis by analysis! In the end he actually ruined the tune he started out with.

Review your work – less is more

Once your idea has been developed and recorded in Cubase SX/SL take time to review it objectively. It's usually best left until the next day or even later. You will see a clearer, fresher picture. Those first ideas, great at the time, may require more work. First ideas are not always the best ideas and you may see ways of improving them. Maybe an introduction will suggest itself out of the general thematic material. Intros are paradoxically best left until the end. When composed first they often end up having nothing to do with what follows. Either that or they remain just great intros that go no further.

One more thing. When reviewing your work look for ways of cutting down on unnecessary details. They can usually be found and a bit of ruthless pruning often yields a leaner but more effective composition. If you can't find any, all well and good, but do ask yourself a few questions like: Am I keeping that clever break because it really works? Or am I keeping it because I can't bear to let it go? Be objective. If a particular ingredient is not serving a definite purpose, get rid of it!

Oh! and for goodness sake don't do what Dave did and start mixing after only eight bars. It happens, I can assure you.

Project 5: a computer game track

Y ou will now follow the creative composition process through using a set brief and applying principles and techniques discussed in previous chapters. The music composed here does not use melodic development to carry it forward, but an additive technique whereby small fragments and cells of material are repeated and transposed to form blocks of material. These blocks are repeated in a loop like fashion and new layers of material are introduced in subsequent cycles to maintain interest. The overall effect is a static one, but that's precisely what is required – atmospheric background music.

Musical objectives

- To build a complete composition with Cubase SX/SL from small fragments and motifs using simple techniques of repetition and harmonic variation.
- Paint an atmospheric musical landscape suitable for background music to match the demands of the assignment.
- Achieve clarity and balance through choice of instruments (timbre) stereo placement and mixing.

Cubase SX/SL skills

- Altering note lengths.
- Changing velocity values.
- Applying Legato.
- Using the Transpose feature.
- Applying compression.
- Repeat Objects and Shared Copies.
- Set up and use of VST instrument – A1 synth.
- Inserting and utilising MIDI controllers Volume, Pan, Reverb and Chorus.
- Inserting and utilising the Reverb B plug-in.

Preparation

1 From the CD, copy the folder named 'project 5' to your desktop.
2 Inside the 'project 5' folder you'll find a file named 'template5.cpr.' Open it and use it for this project.

3 Create a folder in which to save your own files as you work through the project.

The Assignment

OK, here's the scenario. A computer game company has commissioned you to compose the music for a scene in their latest historical title set in Elizabethan times. The piece must run for a minimum of three minutes.

It's night-time and a lone sailor is seen searching a misty quay side for a hidden treasure map. Moored sailing ships bob gently on the tide. Apart from the sailor, the scene is mostly static. Something repetitive is needed to underpin the structure. Start by recording a short ostinato. A simple line on the lower strings of an acoustic guitar will do nicely.

To gain an overall picture, at this point you may prefer to listen to the finished thing rather than let things unfold. To do so, load 5.mix.cpr.

Take 1

Track 1: (chn: 1) Guitar 1.
Quantize Selector: 1/8 Note.
Inspector: [out: GM] [chn: 1] [prg: 25] Nylon String Guitar.
Transport panel: (L) 1.01.01 (R) 5.01.01 Activate AQ.

Guitar parts are usually written an octave higher than they sound, even on a concert score. In this case, as you are probably playing a keyboard, it has been left at concert pitch. Play exactly as written.

1   Record the guitar ostinato. (Figures P5.1 and P5.2) Although it's only a one bar repeated figure, it is better to play it four times in succession. This is better than recording it once and duplicating it because the velocities will be more varied and the result more realistic sounding. Depending on your playing style, the result may sound a little stilted if there is too much of a gap between notes. As you know, plucked guitar strings have a resonant quality and are slow to decay. If this is the case, select the part and open the Key Editor. If it looks anything like Figure P5.3 – the notes do not quite meet each other – select all the notes and apply Legato [MIDI > Functions > Legato] to lengthen them. The notes are now placed end to end and should appear like those in Figure P5.2.
2   Save Project – compare with 5.1.cpr.

Info

Ostinato – a posh word for riff!

Info

The template has a time signature of 4/4 and the tempo is 105 bpm. Now this may be a bit fast for you. If so, turn off the Master tempo and select a bpm value to suit you. When listening back, turn on the Master tempo.

Tip

To add a tough of realism, allow the first note of each bar, A1, to ring through the entire bar.

Figure P5.1 Guitar ostinato.

Figure P5.2 (below) Key Editor view.

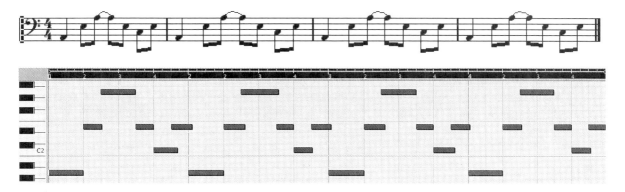

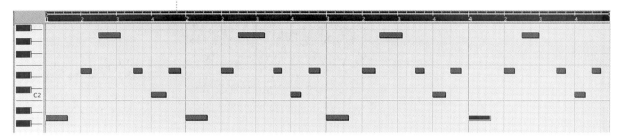

Figure P5.3 Note the gaps between notes.

What next? It's night time and it's misty. How about some minor chords over that riff? Simple triads (three note chords) will do. But a guitar has six strings' I hear you say. True, but this is not a real guitar and six notes will prove too dense for the simple effect needed to create a moody atmosphere. However, if open spaced triads are used they will produce the depth that's needed.

Take 2

Track 2: Guitar 2.
Quantize Selector: 1/8 Note.
Inspector: [out: GM] [chn: 2] [prg: 25] Nylon String Guitar.
Transport panel: (L) 1.01.01 (R) 5.01.01. Activate AQ.

Figure P5.4 Chord sequence.

Figure P5.5 (below) Key Editor view.

1 Record the chord sequence in Figures P5.4 and P5.5.

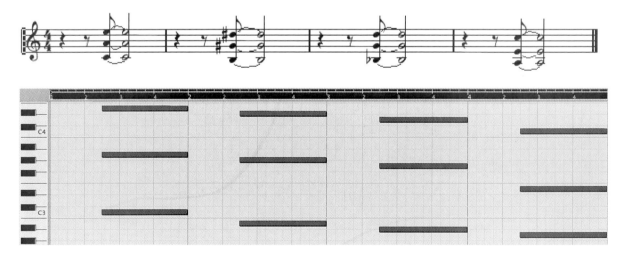

Listen to the result. If any notes sound too short, check them by viewing in the Key Editor. Unlike Guitar 1, the notes need not line up end to end. If any are obviously too short, then lengthen them by grabbing the bottom right-hand corner – a double headed arrow appears – and dragging to the required length. Alternatively, alter the Length value in the Info line (Figure P5.6).

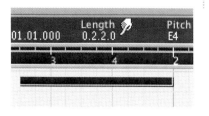

Figure P5.6 Lengthening a note in the Info line.

Info

How much you can lengthen notes depends on the snap value. Turn off Snap with the Snap icon to make fine adjustments (Figure P5.7).

2 Select both recorded parts, and use the Repeat command [Edit > Repeat...] to replicate them once. Leave Shared Copies unchecked.
There are now eight measures of music on tracks 1 and 2 (Guitar 1 & 2).
3 With the Glue tool, join the two parts on track 1 together.
4 Repeat the procedure with the two parts on track 2.
5 Save Project – compare with 5.2a.cpr.

OK so far, so good, but the same eight bars cannot be repeated indefinitely without some form of variation. On the other hand, too much variation will result in overkill. It's a predominately static scene remember. Repeat the same eight bar sequence but drop the pitch a perfect fourth whilst doing so. That way you'll keep the minor chords and retain the moody atmosphere.

1 Select the part on track 1 (bars 1 – 9) and duplicate it between bars 9 and 17.
2 Select the new, copied sequence (9 – 17), and open the Transpose box [MIDI > Transpose...] and enter a value of –5 (Figure P5.8).
3 Repeat the above procedure with the sequence on track 2.

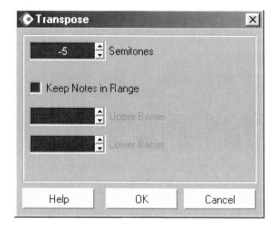

Figure P5.8 MIDI Transpose box.

Set the locators to cycle between (L) 1.01.01 (R) 17.01.01 and play the piece back a couple of times. 'Sounds good to me maestro' (as a well known session bass player was fond of saying to the musical director when he wanted to get home early without doing another take!) 'I'm happy with that.' A look in the editors will reveal the data changes.

4 Save Project – compare with 5.2b.cpr.

There are now 16 bars that can be repeated ad infinitum, as long as interesting variations are dreamt up to overlay.

5 Join the two sequences together on track 1.

6 Repeat the procedure on track 2.

7 Copy and paste the sequences on both tracks (bars 1 – 17) to bar 17.

8 Save Project – compare with 5.2c.cpr.

There are now 32 bars of guitars. A different texture perhaps? Strings come to mind, and movement. A rhythmic figure maybe.

Take 3

Track 3: Strings.
Quantize Selector: 1/8 Note.
Inspector: [out: GM] [chn: 3] [prg: 49].
Transport panel: (L) 17.01.01 (R) 21.01.01. Activate AQ.

Follow these steps:

1 Record the string part (Figures P5.9 and P5.10). Note the accent on the first eighth note in each measure. Play this with slightly more emphasis than the other notes. Visualise the string section bowing this figure and transfer that to your own playing. Imagine yourself actually playing in that string section. It may sound crazy, but that's how it's done! Cubase SX/SL will receive these accented notes at slightly higher velocity values.

Figure P5.9 Strings.

Figure P5.10 Strings, Key Editor view.

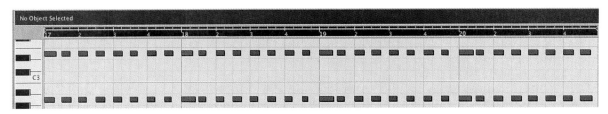

2 Check these velocity values in the Key Editor. Click on a note and use the Info line. If you underplayed the accented notes increase their velocities by scrolling the value in the Info Line (Figure P5.11) .

Figure P5.11 Scrolling velocity value.

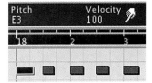

You now have another short ostinato figure ready for repetition and variation.

3 Save Project – compare with 5.3a.cpr.
4 Copy the string part (bars 17 – 21) to bar 21 and glue the two resulting parts together.
5 Copy this new part (bars 17 – 25) to bar 25. Once again there are two string parts.
6 Select the second part (bars 25 – 33) and as you did with the guitars, transpose it down a perfect fourth (–5) in the Transpose box.
7 Select all the parts on all the tracks between bars 17 and 33. Copy them to bar 33. There are now 48 bars of music.
8 Save Project – compare with 5.3b.cpr.

So, a quick review of things so far. You have set a nice background scene through the use of repetitive ostinato figures and limited harmonic variation. Nothing here to distract the game player whilst he noodles around the murky dockyard looking for treasure maps. Even so, to repeat it again would run the risk of sending him to the land of nod. Some melody is needed, but nothing too intrusive. A fragment lasting around four measures would be ideal. Choice of instrument? What about clarinet. Nice and dark when played in the lower register.

Take 4

Track 4: Clarinet.
Quantize Selector: 1/16 Note.
Inspector: [out: GM] [chn: 3] [prg: 72].
Transport panel: (L) 33.01.01 (R) 37.01.01 Activate AQ.

Follow these steps:

1 Record the clarinet part (Figures P5.12 and P5.13). Note the Quantize value has changed to 1/16. This is to accommodate the sixteenth notes at the beginning of the melody. Clarinets are members of the woodwind family and a vibrating wooden reed produces the sound. Clarinet players articulate with their tongue, by striking this reed. Observe the written articulation – legato slurs and staccato notes – when playing the part into Logic.
2 Copy the newly recorded clarinet part (bars 33 – 37) to bar 37 and glue both parts together.
3 Copy the resulting part (bars 33 – 41) to bar 41. Once again, there are two parts.

Figure P5.12 Clarinet.

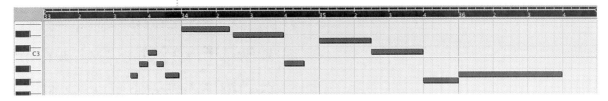

Figure P5.13 Clarinet, Key Editor view.

4 Transpose the second part (bars 41 – 48) down a perfect fourth (-5) using the Transpose box. Incidentally, you have now taken the clarinet below its normal range. No matter. In the real world a bass clarinet would play this part. As the GM sound set does not contain a bass clarinet, transposing the normal clarinet this low is acceptable.

OK, this seems to be working. Copy another 16 bars.

5 Select the sequences between bars 33 and 49 and copy them to bar 49.
6 Save Project – compare with 5.4.cpr.

Something new? I love pizzicato strings used to add that atmospheric touch. You will now add a simple arpeggio figure.

Take 5

Track 5: Pizzicato Strings.
Quantize Selector: 1/8 Note.
Inspector: [out: GM] [chn: 5] [prg: 46].
Transport panel: (L) 49.01.01 (R) 53.01.01. Activate AQ.

Follow these steps:

1 Record the pizzicato strings (Figures P5.14 and P5.15).

Figure P5.14 Pizzicato strings.

Figure P5.15 Pizzicato strings, Key Editor view.

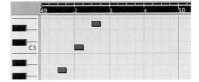

This figure is played at the beginning of the bar, just before the clarinet entry, and therefore avoids any confusion, that may have resulted, had you placed it elsewhere in the four bar cycle.

2 Copy the pizzicato part (bars 49 – 53) to bar 53. Glue the two parts together.
3 Copy the resulting part to bar 57. Once again, There are two parts.

4 Transpose the second part (bars 57 – 65) down a perfect fourth (-5) using the Transpose box.

The musical canvas is filling up nicely but the stereo picture needs sorting out. Final decisions can wait for the moment, so use the Inspector to try out a few preliminary settings.

5 Set the locators between 49 and 65. Enable cycle and play.
6 Using the Pan section in the Inspector, separate the two virtual guitarists by panning the first to a value of –40 and the second to 40. Leave the strings in the centre (C). Place the clarinettist at –16 and the pizzicato strings at 16. You now have quite a nice stereo spread. Have a peek in the Mixer [Devices > Mixer] and you'll notice the changes reflected in the pan settings (Figure P5.16).
7 Set the locators – (L) 49.01.01 (R) 65.01.01, select all parts and copy them to bar 65.
8 Save Project – compare with 5.5.cpr.

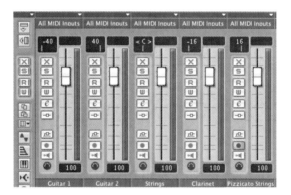

Figure P5.16 Pan settings, Mixer view.

It's all going 'swimmingly' so far and there's room on the canvas for more. Something nautical? A fragment from a well known sea shanty perhaps? The Drunken Sailor obviously! Played on the accordion? Of course!

Take 6

Track 6: Accordion.
Quantize Selector: 1/16 Note.
Inspector: [out: GM] [chn: 6] [prg: 22].
Transport panel: (L) 57.01.01 (R) 61.01.01.

Follow these steps:

1 Record the accordion part (Figures P5.17 and P5.18). This fragment works best over the lower transposed section, hence the Locator positions of 57 – 61.

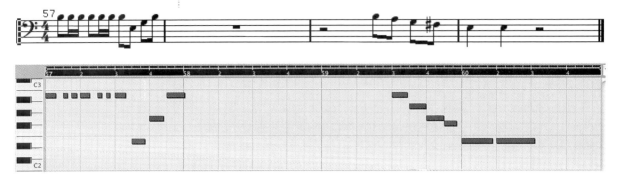

Figure P5.17 Accordion.

Figure P5.18 (top) Accordion, Key Editor view.

2 'What shall we do with the drunken sailor?' – Dump him on the far left! Inspector: pan value –63.
3 Copy the accordion part (bars 57 – 61) to bar 61. Glue the two sequences together.
4 Copy the new accordion sequence to bar 73.
5 Save Project – compare with 5.6.cpr.

I think there's room for a little more nautical nonsense. How about a Hornpipe?

Take 7

Track 7: Piccolo.
Quantize Selector: 1/16 Note.
Inspector: [out: GM] [chn: 7] [prg: 73].
Transport panel: (L) 64.01.01 (R) 66.01.01.

Follow these steps:

1 Record the piccolo part (Figures P5.19 and P5.20). Play it one octave higher than written. This fragment is placed at the end of the clarinet line and just before the pizzicato strings. No confusion.
2 Copy the piccolo part (bars 64 – 66) to bars 68, 72 and 76. There are now four piccolo parts.

Figure P5.19 Piccolo.

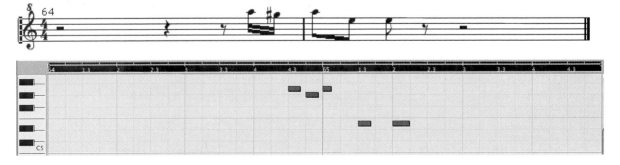

Figure P5.20 Piccolo, Key Editor view .

3 Select the last two parts in turn (bars 72 – 74 and 76 – 78) and transpose them up a fifth by adding a value of 7 (seven semitones) in the Transpose box. Yes, I know everything else went down a fourth, but I fancied a change! It also provides contrast to the other descending parts.
4 Where to place the piccolo player? Over on the right, as far away from the drunken sailor as possible! Pan value 64.
5 Save Project – compare with 5.7.cpr.

At this point I think a couple of special effects would work a treat at instilling yet more atmosphere to this backdrop. GM effects are not noted for their realism but used carefully, in the background, can work quite well. Why not try the Seashore effect? Back to the top!

The Seashore effect – program 123 on the GM sound set varies considerably from one sound module to another. Some are quite convincing and others are plain awful. I hope yours is not like mine, which includes a flock of seagulls!

Take 8

Track 8: Seashore.
Quantize Selector: 1/8 Note.
Inspector: [out: GM] [chn: 8] [prg: 123].
Transport panel: (L) 1.01.01 (R) 9.01.01.

Follow these steps:

1 Record the seashore effect (Figures P5.21 and P5.22). It doesn't matter which note you use. They all play the same sample. I've used middle C. Leave it in the centre (C).
2 Save Project – compare with 5.8.cpr.

Figure P5.21 Seashore.

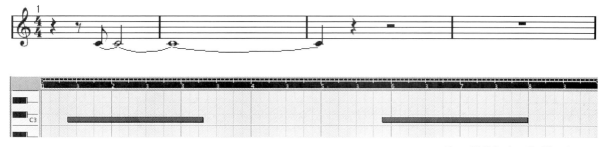

Figure P5.22 Seashore, Key Editor view.

Something else? A ship's bell perhaps. Ghost-like in the mist.

Take 9

> *Track 9:* Tubular-Bell.
> *Quantize Selector:* 1/8 -Note.
> *Inspector:* [out: GM] [chn: 9] [prg: 15].
> *Transport Bar:* (L) 1.01.01 (R) 5.01.01.

Follow these steps:

1 Record the tubular bell (Figures P5.23 and P5.24). It works a treat. Pan it to value 30 for now.
2 Now calculate how many times to repeat the seashore and tubular bell. 72 bars, divided by 8 = 9 times. Use Edit > Repeat … In the resulting dialogue box:

   • Enter 9 for Count.
   • Check the Shared Copies option.

3 Save Project – compare with 5.9.cpr.

Figure P5.23 Tubular bell.

Figure P5.24 Tubular bell, Key Editor view.

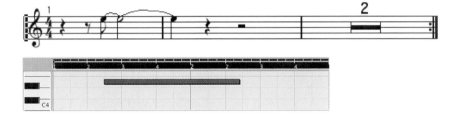

What now? There are now 80 bars of music, a full sound canvas with no room left for any moving parts without the risk of confusing the listener. I still think it needs something else … a pad of some kind … high strings in fifths will create a nice back-

Figure P5.25 The A1 – VST instrument.

drop and sit well with the descending guitar chords. Now it just so happens that Cubase SX/SL's own VST instrument, the A1 is capable of some great pad sounds (Figure P5.25).

Take 10

Track 10: A1.
Quantize Selector: 1/4 – Note.
Inspector: [out: A1] [chn: 1] [prg: Zeitlos SX T].
Transport panel: (L) 1.01.01 (R) 9.01.01.

I have chosen the A1 pre-set called Zeitlos SX T. You may prefer another, or you may want to experiment and edit the chosen pre-set. To do so:

1 Select track 10 and click on the Edit button near the top of the Inspector (Figure P5.26).

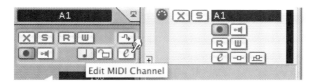

Figure P5.26 Edit button.

2 Choose a pre-set from the drop-down menu (Figure P5.27).

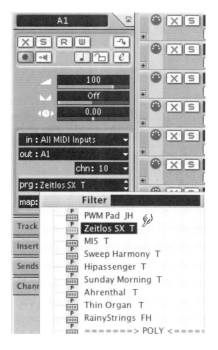

Figure P5.27 A1 – Choosing pre-sets.

Now follow these steps:

1 Select track 10 and record the string pad (Figures P5.28 and P5.29). Play these gently. If you find it difficult to do so, try reducing or compressing the velocities in the Track Parameters.

Figure P5.28 String pad.

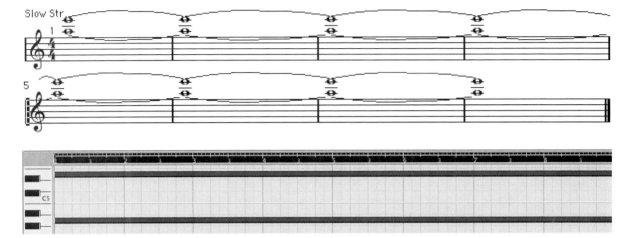

Figure P5.29 String pad, Key Editor view.

Tip

Adding compression before you play reduces the velocity as you play.

2 Copy the part (bars 1 – 9) to bar 9.

3 Transpose the new part (bars 9 – 17) down a perfect fourth (-5) using the Transpose box [MIDI > Transpose]. Glue the two Parts together.

4 Copy the new part (bars 1 – 17) to bar 17 and through to the end of the piece [Edit > Repeat ... x4].

5 Glue all the sequences on track 10 together.

6 To make the string line continuous:

    A   select the track and open the Key Editor.

    B   select all the notes [Edit > Select > All].

    C   apply Legato [MIDI > Functions > Legato.

7 Save Project – compare with 5.10.cpr.

OK, there are now eighty bars, just over three minutes long. Time to end it. If used with a game it probably wouldn't need one. But what the hell! I like endings. How about a very simple one note ending on the Guitar 1 track?

Take 11

Track 2: Guitar 2.
Quantize Selector: 1/4 Note.
Inspector: [out: GM]: [chn: 2] [prg: 25.
Transport Bar: (L) 81.01.01 (R) 83.01.01.

Follow these steps:

1   Record the guitar (Figure P5.30 and P5.31).
2   Save Project – compare with 5.11.cpr.

Figure P5.30 Guitar.

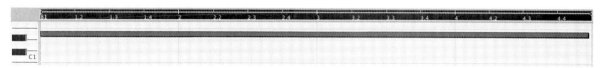

Figure P5.31 Guitar, Key Editor view.

The mix

Mixing this piece is straightforward enough, but beware, it's easy to get carried away, especially with the comprehensive mixing facilities now available with Cubase SX/SL. I have learned through experience to use effects and signal processing sparingly.

Everybody does it differently, but I like to get the stereo picture and volume levels clear before I decide to add effects. Up to now I have left volume at a value of 100 in the Instrument Parameter box. Before changing them I listened back and decided to alter the stereo picture slightly.

Pan settings

The guitars were a little too far apart and unbalanced as a result. They were brought closer together. Guitar 1 (–20) and Guitar 2 (20).

The Clarinet was competing for space with the Accordion, so I moved it to the right (16). The pizzicato strings have changed sides (–16). They enter after the clarinet, which is on the right, and I wanted a contrast, on the left.

Volume levels

I used the Mixer to play around with the volume levels until I found a suitable balance. The main thing to remember here is to keep the A1 pad fairly low to begin with. Think of it as a backdrop, a kind of musical canvas on which the other instruments are painted, one at a time. As each one appears it should sound clear and detailed against the backdrop, but never too dominant. I ended up with the settings in Figure P5.32. Yours of course will be different.

Figure P5.32 Mixer settings.

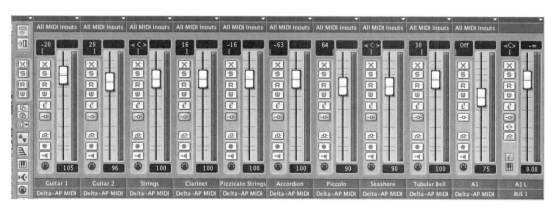

Reverb settings

That settled, I listened again. The obvious candidate for reverberation was the 'Seashore' sound. It needed more ambience. I set this at 95 for a distant effect.

For the remaining GM sounds I used a value of 55. Any more would have robbed them of detail and muddied the mix. These settings were made using an Insert on specific channels – read the mix instructions in project 3 for instructions on how to do this – and work fine for my GM sound module but may be unsuitable for yours. Make your own judgements and adjustments.

Now for the A1 synth. To add reverberation to the pre-set:

1   Made sure the Show/Hide VST Instrument Channels button was activated in the Mixer (Figure P5.33). This gave me access to the VST Instrument Channel Strip (Figure P5.34).

Figure P5.33 Show/Hide VST Instrument Channels.

2   From the drop-down menu, selected Inserts (Figure P5.35).
3   In the top slot – Insert 1 – selected Reverb B (Figure P5.36).
4   Pressed the edit button revealing the effect itself and chose the Sci-Fi pre-set (Figure P5.37), an odd choice for Elizabethan times, I know, but it sounds good and that's all that matters to me!
5   Adjusted the reverberation Mix to 80%, I wanted it nice and wet.

None of the above took as long as it takes to read! It's quite easy when you get the hang of it.

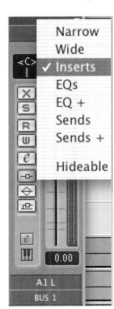

Figure P5.36 Selecting Insert Effect.

Figure P5.34 VST Instrument Channel Strip

Figure P5.35 Selecting Inserts.

Figure P5.37 Choosing Effect pre-set.

Chorus

I decided the guitar would benefit from judicious use of a chorus effect. All right, I know they didn't have digital effects processors back in Sir Francis Drake's day, but who cares! It serves the purpose of beefing things up a little. I set a value of 35 which worked fine on my GM sound module. It'll no doubt be different for yours.

The result? I'm happy. There's always another way to do it but part of doing this kind of thing for a living is deciding when to stop. Time's money. Commitments have to be made. No doubt you would do it another way.

Open 5.mix. Go ahead! Experiment! That's how you learn but don't even think about altering it and claiming copyright – I have a brilliant lawyer!

A look at musical form

Practically all music has form – a structure or framework, often planned before the composition process even begins. I'm referring here to composed music as opposed to improvised music (although improvisation is often based on form anyway). The casual listener does not always notice the form, nor should they because in most cases it's a hidden element. They enjoy the music on a superficial level, and quite rightly so. After all, when we gaze at a work of art we are not necessarily examining its hidden form. We appreciate the whole picture.

Sometimes the musical form is very simple and glaringly obvious, the twelve bar blues being a perfect example. Other times it's very complicated and stretched across a long time span. A classical symphony, for instance, may contain four complete movements and last up to forty-five minutes or more.

One thing's for sure. Although the listener may not be consciously aware of musical form they certainly know when it's missing! Formless music – and plenty has been composed and forgotten – lacks the sense of completeness which is perceived by the listener and held in their memories. Of course good music has been written without conventional musical form but it has no place in this book which is primarily concerned with producing commercial music.

Form can be anything you want it to be. It's about organisation. However, over time, certain musical forms have appeared and remained embedded in popular culture. They've stood the test of time and provided a basic structure for composers to use repeatedly. Take a quick look at some established musical forms in three very different genres on the CD.

Tip

To examine the Cubase SX/SL files for this chapter, copy the folders named 'form' and 'exile' from the CD to your computer.

Simple three part forms

A simple three part form is referred to as ABA. The third section is a recapitulation of the first, sometimes harmonically and melodically modified. The middle section is a contrast to avoid monotony.

Follow these steps:

1 Load form/haydn.cpr and view the Project window (Figure 4.1).
2 Set the MIDI output to your GM sound source.

This extract is from a Haydn Piano Sonata (Figure 4.2). Track 1 contains the right hand parts and track 2 the left. You will notice that the Marker contains a reference to the form. Section A is sixteen bars long. It is in fact an eight bar segment played twice. An analogy: think of A as the home page on a themed Internet site. B is a con-

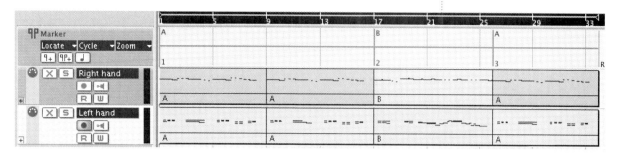

trasting section and consists of nine bars. The rhythmic structure and phrasing are similar to the A section but the harmony sets it apart. The scenery is familiar but we've definitely left the home page. The piece finishes with a note for note repetition of A. Back home! It would be more accurately described as an A A B A structure.

Figure 4.1 haydn.cpr.

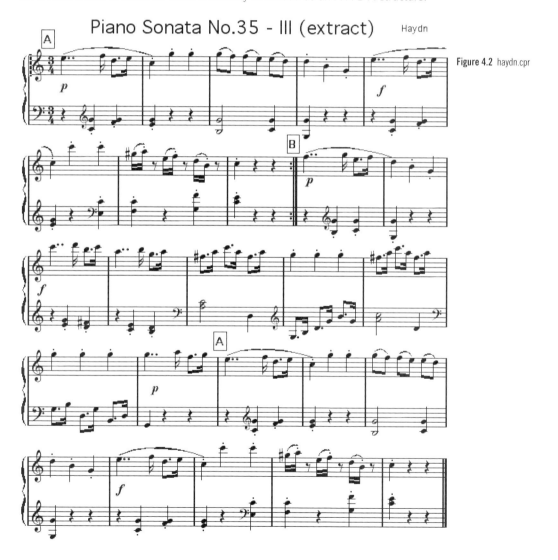

Figure 4.2 haydn.cpr

Here's another example. Follow these steps:

1 Load form/minuet.cpr. This one's from Bach's French Suite (Figure 4.3).
2 Set the MIDI output to your GM sound source.

Again the A section is followed by a contrasting B section. However, in this example the recapitulation has been varied. The reason? Well, A ends on the dominant and sounds incomplete. Bach needed an ending. He begins the recapitulation the same (for two bars) but then leads us home to the tonic in the last bar. The Marker track shows this structure as A1, B and A2.

Figure 4.3 minuet.cpr.

Jazz standards

Jazz musicians often use the classic standard song repertoire from the first half of the twentieth century for their improvisations. *I Got Rhythm* by Gershwin is a typical example. Although in a completely different style from the minuet above its form is basically the same: A A B A. Here's a tune in a similar style called *Raising Standards*.

Follow these steps:

1 Load form/raisings.cpr (Figure 4.4).
2 Set the MIDI output to your GM sound source.

The Marker shows the form. Section A1 and A2 are both eight bars long. The difference between them lies in bars 15 and 16, in the A2 section, where the melody and harmony have been modified. Section B is a contrasting section, generally referred to by jazz musicians as the 'bridge'. The tune finishes with eight bars of A3. Again, things have been changed slightly to bring about the ending.

Figure 4.4 raisings.cpr.

Pop songs

Pop songs are varied in their structure. However one form seems to be more predominant than most. A verse followed by a chorus is repeated two or three times and contrasted with a bridge. This gives way once again to the verse and chorus. Sometimes the bridge is used again. This corresponds to an A B A B C A B structure. Here's an example.

Follow these steps:

1 Load exile/exile.cpr and view the Project window (Figure 4.5).
2 Set the MIDI output to your GM sound source.

This tune, although an instrumental, follows the format of many a rock song in its construction. Medieval in character it could have been played by an electric folk band from the seventies such as *Fairport Convention*.

It kicks off with a verse (A) lasting fourteen bars followed by an eight bar chorus (B). The verse and chorus are then repeated. This takes us up to bar 42. To repeat things again would be bordering on the tedious so a ten bar bridge is introduced for relief (C). Now that could have led straight back to either the verse or chorus, (as it does in millions of songs) but in this case the bridge has been extended by adding another eight bar section (D). This helps build a sense of expectancy. The verse returns and is followed by a chorus and ending. This is then, an A B A B C D A B structure.

It's a good idea to have a basic form in mind before starting a composition. Although you will probably modify it as you write the piece, jotting down a simple structure first will serve as a guide.

Figure 4.5 Exile.cpr.

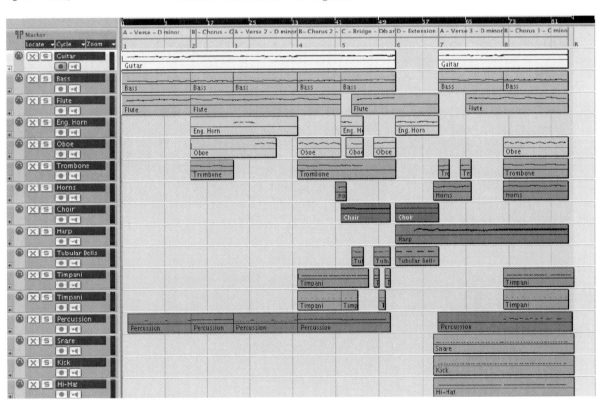

The building blocks of composition

In Chapter 1, MIDI Sequencing, I explained how technically challenged keyboard players, like myself, can record a difficult piece of music by breaking it down into manageable chunks. We dismantle the composition, piece by piece and rebuild it again as sequencing objects on a track in the Project window within Cubase. You could liken this process to a building being dismantled and reassembled, brick by brick, in a new location. There is much to be learned by doing this and Cubase SX/SL is an ideal place to do it because we can see the constituent parts, or building blocks of a composition clearly displayed in the Project window.

The phrase

You probably discovered earlier, when sequencing three completely different styles of music, that musical common sense prompted you to play and record the music as complete phrases. We can assume then, that a phrase is the smallest structural unit used for composition. It has a sense of completeness. It can be sung or played in a single breath and has a definite beginning and ending.

Follow these steps:

1 Load exile/exile.cpr and view the flute (track 3) in the Score window. The first phrase is marked 'Question'. It's a complete unit. Think of it as a musical sentence. Better still, think of it as a musical question. It's followed by another phrase, the 'Answer'.
2 Look through and play the score to identify other such phrases. What do these phrases consist of? What is the main ingredient? Well melody for a start. For me, this is usually the most important part of the creative process. The melody comes first and the rest follows later.

Melody

OK, not all music relies on melody but the overwhelming majority does. How many times have you heard a snatch of melody and it's instant recall time? You know exactly where it came from. Even if you can't remember where its origins lie, the damn thing nags you silly until you eventually find out. That's the power of melody. That recall will often bring to mind a particular memory. It may well bring submerged emotions to the surface. Powerful stuff!

What constitutes a melody? At its most basic, a string of notes which rise and fall. But that's not enough.

Follow these steps:

Figure 5.1 oddnotes.cpr.

1 Load blocks/oddnotes.cpr (Figure 5.1).
2 Set the MIDI output to your GM sound source.
3 Listen to this group of notes. Not very memorable, is it?
4 Now load blocks/igetit .cpr (Figure 5.2). It's the same order of notes, but what a transformation. It's instantly recognisable as *Eine Kleine Nacht Musik* by Mozart, an absolute master of melody. What brought about the transformation? The rhythm. Without a rhythmic shape the melody does not exist.

Figure 5.2 igetit.cpr.

What else constitutes a melody? A distinctive shape, brought about by the pitch of the notes as a melody unfolds. A string of adjacent notes soon becomes monotonous without a leap – large or small, up or down – of some kind.

Take another look at the first few phrases of Exile (exile/exile.cpr). Now this is a gentle melody, nothing very dramatic, which gradually climbs a scale. To make it a little more interesting there is a leap of a fourth between the first two notes (A and D). Each time the melody climbs a step there is a return to the A before leaping back up again and continuing the ascent.

High climax points within the melodic shape are also important for emotional intensity. In this case the highest note arrives at the beginning of each chorus.

Low notes can have the opposite effect and are often used to calm things down. The English horn does just that between bars 52 and 60 (track 4).

A good melody can be likened to well written prose. A readable page of text contains clearly defined phrases and frequent use of punctuation. Bear this in mind when writing melodies. Time taken crafting a memorable melody is time well spent.

Harmony

A vast subject which needs a complete book of its own. In fact there are several excellent books available. If you're into composing and arranging – you must be if you bought this book – I'm assuming that you already have a basic knowledge of the subject. However, I can supply a few guidelines.

Beginning composers working with Cubase or similar sequencers often make the mistake of attempting to write a chord sequence and melody together. It doesn't usually work! Not many people can control all these elements at once, not least a beginner. The usual result of this way of writing is either a few measures of block chords following every single melody note with the bass playing only root notes or a few measures of repetitive chords and a boring melody line. Everything grinds to a halt pretty soon after. It's a very common mistake and simply the result of trying to think of two things (sometimes three if rhythm is included) at once.

It's far easier to get the melody down first. It's what people are going to remember after all. Craft the melody, make it interesting, and add chords afterwards. You will discover that a melody often suggests the harmony anyway.

It depends on the style of music of course, but when you add the harmony avoid having the bass constantly following the chords in root position. One way to get a more interesting harmonic structure is through careful construction of the bass line. Make it distinctive. Give it a life of its own and where possible, and appropriate, have it move in the opposite direction to the melody. This will nearly always give a good result. This movement inevitably provides interesting inversions and passing notes.

Follow these steps:

1 Load exile/dullbass.cpr
2 Set the MIDI output to your GM sound source and play it through. The guitar is playing this chord sequence:

Dm / A7 / | Dm / / / | Dm / A7 / | Dm / / / |

F / Gm / | Am / / / | C / E7 / | Am / / / ||

The chords are OK, simple yes, but it's a rather plaintive melody and doesn't need complicated chords. Not quite right though, is it? How can we make it more harmonically interesting?

3 Switch to exile/exile.cpr (the previous song) and play the opening measures. By having the bass move, for the most part, in the opposite direction to the melody we have created the following:

Dm / A7 / | Dm7 / / Bbmaj7 | Dm / A7 / | Dm / / Gm9 |
    C#   C   A

F / Gm7 / | Fmaj7 / / / | C / E7 / | Am / Am / ||
   F   B   C

That's better. The bass is now playing a kind of counter melody – appropriate here because the drums have yet to enter – and created several inversions, new chords and interesting passing notes along the way.

Modulation is another way to make the harmonic structure interesting. It's often best to write what the melody suggests and the modulation should be smooth and natural sounding. The listener will not consciously perceive these key changes – but their subconscious will.

Exile is a simple enough song but helped along the way with several key changes. You can see them indicated in the Marker:

The verse is in D minor, the chorus in G minor and the bridge uses D flat major and A major. The bridge extension returns to D minor. These modulations are the direct result of the melody. Not the other way around.

Info

Modulation is the changing from one key to another within a composition.

Rhythm

Another vast subject. We have seen how a rhythmic design can change an ordinary string of notes into a memorable tune. Its most important role though is in the accompaniment. It can probably be best studied in piano music, where it is usually evident in the left hand part.

Most instrumental music used in the commercial world, makes extensive use of rhythm in the accompaniment, usually drums and percussion and is often derived from the character of the melody. For example, I wrote the melody for Exile before adding rhythm and harmony. The melody suggested both.

Take another look at the melody in the beginning phrase and you will notice that the first nine notes are eighth notes (quavers). Pretty straightforward stuff that, to my ears, suggested a classic rock drum rhythm (Figures 5.3 and 5.4) used on countless recordings over the last four or five decades. Simple but effective. Of course we all hear things differently and had that melody been written by someone else (you?) the rhythmic scheme may well have taken a different turn.

Figure 5.3 Rock rhythm.

Figure 5.4 Rock rhythm, Drum Editor view.

Pitch	Instrument	6 1	2	3	4
C1	Bass Drum	◇		◇ ◇	
C#1	Side Stick				
D1	Acoustic Snare		◆		◆
D#1	Hand Clap				
E1	Electric Snare				
F1	Low Floor Tom				
F#1	Closed Hi-Hat	◇ ◇	◇ ◇	◇ ◇	◇ ◇

Of course rhythmic accompaniment need not be restricted solely to drums. It is very easy to create rhythm in Cubase without the use of percussion sounds. Rhythm can be generated with absolute accuracy using synthesised sounds to play arpeggios and other percussive patterns. These take on a more pulsating effect than the humanly played equivalent. For example, in Exile the drums don't appear until the third verse. However an eighth note pulse has been implied by the guitar arpeggios, (track 1) which also happen to supply the harmony. This is reinforced by a 16th note arpeggio pattern played by the harp (track 9) on the last verse and chorus.

Techno and dance music is playing an increasing role in music for the media. Melody is a secondary consideration in this style of music and the composition process would probably start from the bottom up, with rhythmic patterns and loops being created first.

Melody making

In the previous chapter you used small melodic fragments to build a kind of musical collage suitable for background use. The fragments remained undeveloped. In this chapter you'll learn how small fragments of melody can be expanded into larger structures. In other words constructing a melody.

'Construct a melody!' I can hear you saying, 'surely melodies aren't constructed but revealed, in moments of divine inspiration, to extremely gifted musical people like, Mozart, Irving Berlin, Lennon and McCartney and the like. Not ordinary people like us.

Not so. The first ideas are often inspirational but the hard work of building and constructing soon takes over. As usual it's one percent brain wave, 99 percent hard slog. So you're in with a chance.

So how's it done? Well, there are no hard and fast rules. However, there are some guidelines and general principles that have worked well over the last few hundred years or so. Why do we remember certain melodies, and not others? In most cases we remember the well crafted ones that are carefully developed from a few distinctive ideas. These ideas, are then repeated and varied to form a complete melody. The two key ingredients are repetition and variation. Without repetition the listener has nothing to hold on to and soon becomes bewildered. Without variation boredom sets in.

Cell construction

Don't be frightened of repetition. Without it nobody will be likely to remember anything you compose. A good way of getting started on developing and constructing melodies is to write a short motif or phrase, repeat it several times and introduce variations in pitch. Here is a melody constructed this way (Figures 6.1 and 6.2)

Info

To examine the Cubase files for this chapter, copy the folders named 'cells' and 'exile' from the CD to your computer.

Figure 6.1 Motif cells.

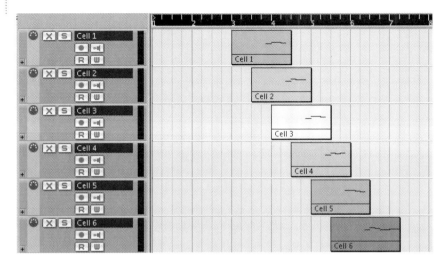

After creating a short motif, I duplicated it five times and varied the pitches of the notes each time, to form a continuous flowing melody. I used several tracks, for clarity, but of course, it could all be done on a single track!

Follow these steps:

1 Load cells/cells.cpr.
2 Set the MIDI output to your GM sound source.
3 Examine the sequences one by one.

Figure 6.2 Motif cells, staff.

- Cell 1: The so-called inspirational beginning. Although it ends on the tonic (it's in the key of F) it has an air of expectancy about it which suggests continuation.
- Cell 2: By raising the pitch of all but the first note I was able to create a new phrase. The air of expectancy continues. We are climbing.

- Cell 3: Another copy is added. The pitches are raised and the climbing continues.
- Cell 4: ... and continues
- Cell 5: We begin a descent.
- Cell 6: This time the motif is extended to complete a musical sentence.

Musical questions and answers

Another way of developing melody is to create musical statements that suggest an answer. The melody for Exile was constructed this way.

Follow these steps:

1 Load exile/exile.cpr.
2 Set the MIDI output to your GM sound source.
3 Take a look at the beginning of the flute part in Exile. The opening phrase (Question 1) poses a kind of musical question that begs an answer. The answer follows in the next phrase (Answer) 1). Although different to Question 1 – note how it rises higher in response – the last five notes are a recall of the last five notes of Question 1. Already there's repetition with a slight variation (Figure 6.3).

Tip

If you are stuck for an idea, try constructing a small rhythmic framework and experiment with various pitch combinations.

Figure 6.3 Exile.

The next phrase (Question 2) follows the same rhythmic pattern as Question 1 but the notes are completely different. That air of expectancy has been fulfilled and a new question asked. Answer 2 answers the question and is a varied repetition of Answer 1.

All this often comes naturally, without thinking. I have merely analysed it. However, if you're stuck for ideas this is a sure fire method of keeping things moving. There are so many ways to achieve this onward flow that a whole book is needed on the subject. You can though, learn a great deal by taking time to listen and analyse other melodies in this way. Reading music, although helpful, is not always necessary.

Audio recording

The next project in the book incorporates the use of a pre-recorded audio track containing an improvised saxophone solo behind the main tune. This can be replaced with another instrument or a vocal track. At this point then, it seems appropriate to have a quick look at the basic audio recording procedure and microphone techniques needed to do this. If you don't happen to play an acoustic instrument and can't stand to hear the sound of your own voice use a synthesised sound instead!

Recording vocals

To record vocals a directional mic mounted on a stand is the usual method and the singer will most likely be standing. If you have a wobbly wooden floor, isolate the stand from the floor to prevent low frequency rumble travelling up the mic stand and on to your recordings. If you can afford it, a condenser mic is best – AKG C-414, AKG C-3000 or the Audio Technica are good – but a dynamic mic such as the trusty Shure SM57 or SM58 will still produce good results.

Although most vocal mics have built-in wind shields it is still a good idea to use a pop screen. There are several types on the market these days. Apart from preventing sudden pops, if you are recording a vocalist other than yourself, it will also prevent them getting too close to the microphone.

A distance of between 15 and 60 cms between the mouth and microphone is usual, depending on the strength and character of the vocalist, with the mic tilted slightly, either up or down, away from a direct line with the mouth. A greater distance is fine but bear in mind the fact that more gain may be needed and if the vocalist has a quiet voice problems with noise could arise. Keep the mic away from reflective surfaces, walls being an obvious example.

Recording electric guitars

A dynamic mic such as the Shure SM58 is the usual choice for the job. To begin with place it between 15 and 30 cms from the centre of one of the speakers in the amp cabinet. Experiment by moving it off centre from there to alter the tone. Try using two mics, one further away or at the side, or even behind the speaker cabinet. Use a similar method for bass guitar, but place it further away to avoid a boxy sound.

Recording acoustic guitars

A directional mic is best, preferably a condenser type, however reasonably good results can still be achieved with a dynamic mic. Position it about 45 cms from the sound hole. Avoid the temptation to place it any closer unless you want a boomy sound.

Recording brass and woodwind

The SM57 will do the job, but a better choice is a condenser mic. Where you place the mic depends very much on where most of the sound comes from, brass from the bell, saxes from the main body of the instrument as well as the bell, flute from the mouthpiece etc. However, particularly with woodwinds, the sound emanates from different parts of the instrument and it is better to keep the mic at a reasonable distance from the player.

Recording strings

Treat individual stringed instruments such as violin in the same way as the acoustic guitar. If you are fortunate enough to have the space and recording a small string ensemble use two mics suspended above the players mounted at right angles to each other for a good stereo image.

From microphone to audio track – the signal route

OK, you are all set to record that blistering solo but how do you actually get the audio signal into Cubase? If you are new to recording and find it confusing, here's a summary of the main things to do using, in the main, the Project window.

1 Connect the audio signal from your external mixer to the audio card input.
2 Open the VST inputs window [Devices > VST Inputs] and ensure that the inputs of your audio card are activated (Figure 7.1).

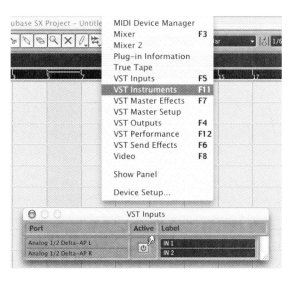

Figure 7.1 VST Inputs.

3 In the Project window, select an audio track and rename it with a relevant name. This makes it easy to identify the recorded files in the Pool and the Mixer.

4 In the Inspector, choose an input in the Input Routing box (Figure 7.2).

5 Decide upon either a stereo or mono track and change it accordingly (Figure 7.3).

6 Arm the track by activating the Record Enable button (Figure 7.4).

Figure 7.2 Choosing inputs.

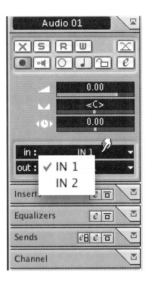

Figure 7.3 Setting mono or stereo tracks.

Figure 7.4 Arming tracks.

7 Adjust the input level using your external mixer or your sound card's software mixer. Too high a signal will show red in the Output activity indicator.

8 Record the audio using the Transport panel, as you do with MIDI tracks.

The recorded audio files can be seen in the Pool [Project > Pool]. The above procedure can of course be performed in the Mixer.

Project 6: a football theme

Musical objectives

- Construct a melody from a small melodic 'cell' by applying repetition and pitch variation.
- Compose a rhythmic bass part to compliment the newly invented melody and consider the harmonic possibilities this implies.
- Use three part sectional harmony to build a 'brass section'.
- Use tenor sax or other instrument to provide an improvised solo behind the main melody.

Cubase SX/SL skills

- Recording an audio track.
- Project Setup – choosing a File Type, Sample Rate and Record Format.
- Using the Stereo switch.
- Input signal routing and level adjustment.
- Record enable audio tracks.
- Understanding audio files and events.
- Punch in/Punch out recording.
- Applying Reverb B as a Send Effect.
- Lengthening and altering the pitch of notes.

Preparation

1 From the CD, copy the folder named 'project 6' to your desktop.
2 Inside the 'project 6' folder you'll find a file named 'template6.cpr.' Open it and use it for this project.
3 Create a folder in which to save your own files as you work through the project.

The assignment

You have been commissioned to compose a one minute theme for a football program. It must be upbeat in tempo, attention grabbing, and uplifting in character.

To gain an overall picture, at this point you may prefer to listen to the finished thing rather than let things unfold. To do so, load 6.mix.cpr.

Take 1

Info

The template has a time signature of 4/4 and the tempo is 140 bpm. Now this may be a bit fast for you. If so scroll the tempo to suit you. When listening back, scroll back to 140 bpm.

Track 1: Trumpet 1
Quantize Selector: 1/8 Sw-50%.
Inspector: [out: GM] [chn: 1] [prg: 62] Brass.
Transport panel: (L) 1.01.01 (R) 3.01.01 Activate AQ.

A blank Project window presents a daunting prospect. But wait – an initial fragment of melody has presented itself and stubbornly sticks in the mind, refusing to go away (Figures P6.1 and P6.2). Record it and take it from there. I've chosen a brass synth sound to get that 'uplifting' quality. To achieve a loose march feel, I've created a swing groove of 1/8 Sw-50% in the Quantize setup box. This has been added to the pre-set menu. The result of the chosen groove can be seen in the List Editor. Note how all the offbeat eighth notes are delayed by forty ticks (Figure P6.3).

Figure P6.1 A fragment of melody.

Figure P6.2 (above) A fragment of melody, Key Editor view.

Figure P6.3 Delayed eighth notes.

L	Type	Start	End
	Note	0001.03.03.040	0001.03.04.067
♩	Note	0001.04.01.000	0001.04.02.049
♩	Note	0001.04.03.044	0002.01.01.003
♩	Note	0002.01.01.000	0002.01.04.077
♩	Note	0002.02.01.000	0002.02.03.008
♩	Note	0002.02.03.044	0003.02.01.060

•   Save Project – compare with 6.1a.cpr.

The plan here is to construct a theme by repeating this fragment and applying variation to it in the various editors.

First , repeat the part seven times [Edit > Repeat...]. There is now a 16 bar section comprised of eight two-bar parts to work on. I shall refer to these parts as Cells 1 – 8 (Figure P6.4).

Here's what you do: (Figures P6.5 and P6.6).

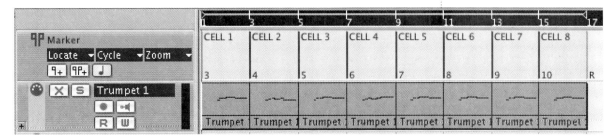

Figure P6.4 Cells 1 – 8.

1 Cell 1: bars (1 – 3): Although it ends on the tonic (it's in the key of Bb) it definitely suggests continuation so:

2 Cell 2: (bars 3 – 5): By keeping the rhythmic framework of Cell 1 intact and altering the pitch of the notes you will generate more melody. Alter the pitch of the notes as shown by using either the Score or Key Editors.

Figure P6.5 Cells 1 – 4, Staff.

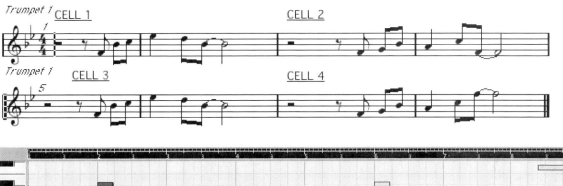

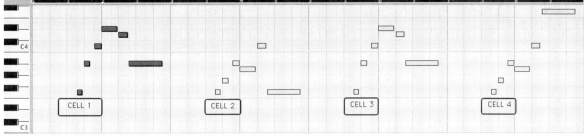

Figure P6.6 Cells 1 – 4, Key Editor view.

3 Cell 3: (bars 5 – 7): The initial phrase can be repeated again without risk of boredom so leave it untouched.

4 Cell 4: (bars 7 – 9): This time use the same note pattern as Cell 2 but raise the last note by an octave. This really does suggest continuation. Upwards! The brief stated uplifting, remember?

5 Save Project – compare with 6.1b.cpr.

Figure P6.7 Use the info bar to change pitch.

When altering the pitch of notes by dragging them up or down in the Score and Key Editors notes are easily moved out of position by mistake. Using the Info bar to change their pitch will avoid this problem (Figure P6.7).

Info

Activating Snap whilst moving notes will allow you to drag them to the specified Quantize value.

Tip

If you want to hear the pitch of a note whilst moving, activate the speaker icon on the toolbar.

After saving the project, continue with Cells 5 – 8 (Figure P6.8 and P6.9).

1 Cell 5: (bars 9 – 11) Change the notes to continue the ascent to C and have the melody fall from there.
2 Cell 6: (bars 11 – 13) Our listeners are unconsciously expecting yet another fall in pitch and a repetition of the familiar rhythmic pattern, but this time, surprise them by applying the brakes. Delete the first three notes – in the Score or Key Editors – and replace them with a half note (minim) half a beat earlier than expected, and continue the descent.
3 Cell 7: (bars 13 – 15) Hover around a bit …
4 Cell 8: (bars 15 – 17) … before landing back on the tonic, where things began.
5 Save Project – compare with 6.1c.cpr.

Figure P6.8 Cells 5 – 8, Staff.

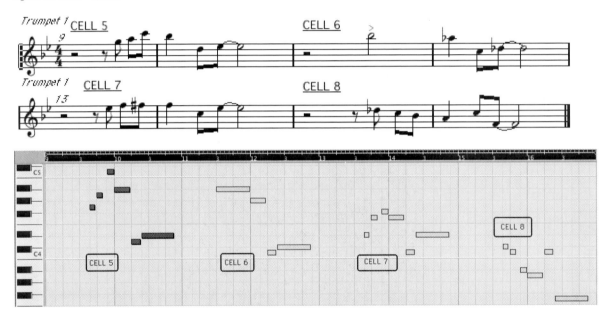

Figure P6.9 Cells 5 – 8, Key Editor view.

Play it through. I think the last note in each cell should be a bit longer by a couple of beats. Now there are several ways to do this. Perhaps the easiest is to select them in the Key Editor and change them together.

Follow these steps:

1 In the Project window, select all the parts [Edit > Select > All on Selected Tracks].
2 Open the Key Editor, and with Snap turned off, select all eight occurrences of the note and drag their lengths to about double size (Figure P6.10).
3 In the Project window, lengthen the last part – Cell 8 (bars 15 – 17) – by one bar to accommodate the longer note, just created, and glue all the parts together.
4 Save Project – compare with 6.1d.cpr.

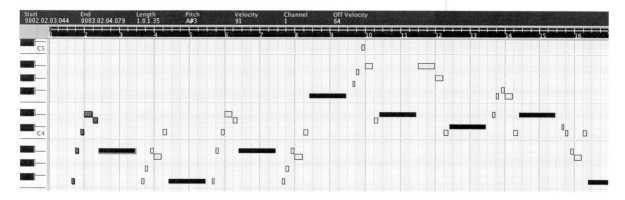

What next? Well it obviously needs a pretty lively rhythm but all I can hear at the moment (mentally) is a four-to-the-bar bass drum. The LM-7 virtual drum machine supplied with Cubase SX/SL will be ideal here. I chose the 909 kit (Figure P6.11).

Figure 6.10 Lengthening notes.

Figure 6.11 The LM-7, 909 kit.

Take 2

Track 7: Kick Drum.
Quantize Selector: 1/8 Note.
Inspector: [out: lm-7] [chn: 10] [prg: 909].
Transport panel: (L) 2.01.01 (R) 6.01.01 Activate AQ.

Follow these steps:

1 Record the four bars of kick drum (C1) (Figure P6.12, P6.13 and P6.14) and using Repeat Events, copy the resulting part three times to complete 16 bars [Edit > Repeat...]. In the resulting dialogue box, enter 'Count: 3' and tick the Shared Copies box (Figure P6.15).

Figure P6.12 (right) Kick drum.

Figure P6.13 Kick drum, Key Editor view.

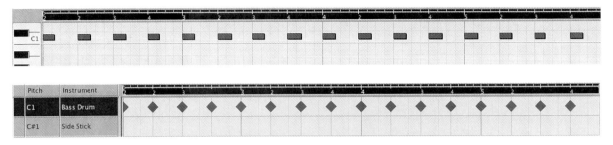

Figure P6.14 (above) Kick drum, Drum Editor view.

Info

Shared copies are linked. Alter one part and you automatically change the others too. Shared copies have their part names indicated with italic text and an icon in the lower right corner.

Figure P6.15 Repeat Events/Shared Copies

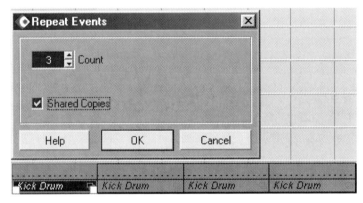

2 Save Project – compare with 6.2.cpr

A bass line is needed. Because of the drum machine style kick drum, a bass synth sound suggests itself. Time to launch the A1 synth again. This time the pre-set is Mono -> Bass T (Figure P6.16).

Figure P6.16 Pre-set is Mono -> Bass T.

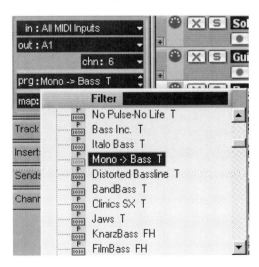

Take 3

Track 6: Bass.
Quantize Selector: 1/8 Note.
Inspector: [out: A1] [chn: 6] [prg: Mono -> Bass T].
Transport panel: (L) 2.01.01 (R) 18.01.01 Activate AQ.

Follow these steps:

1 Record the bass (Figures P6.17 and P6.18). Breaking it down into four bar cycles is favourite! Probably the easiest way. Note bars 6 – 10 are a repeat of bars 2 – 6, so copying that will save time. The choice of notes for the first eight bars (2 – 10) are pretty straightforward stuff. Tonic to Dominant etc. Things get more interesting in bars 10 – 16 where chromatic movement is beginning to suggest more adventurous harmony.
2 Save Project – compare with 6.3.cpr.

Figure P6.17 Bass.

Figure P6.18 Bass, Key Editor view.

Take 4

Track 2: Trumpet 2.
Quantize Selector: 1/8 Sw-50%.
Inspector: [out: GM] [chn: 2] [prg: 62].
Transport panel: (L) 2.01.01 (R) 18.01.01 Activate AQ.

Follow these steps:

1 Record trumpet 2 (Figures P6.19 and P6.20). Break it down if necessary. It's a harmony part and you'll examine it closer after the next track is recorded.

2 Save Project – compare with 6.4.cpr.

Figure P6.19 Trumpet 2.

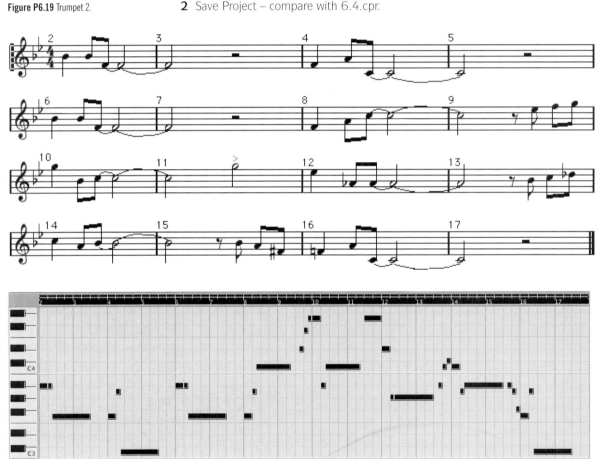

Figure P6.20 Trumpet 2, Key Editor view.

Take 5

Track 3: Trumpet 3.
Quantize Selector: 1/8 Sw-50%.
Inspector: [out: GM] [chn: 3] [prg: 62].
Transport panel: (L) 2.01.01 (R) 18.01.01 Activate AQ.

Follow these steps:

1 Record trumpet 3 (Figure P6.21 and P6.22). Break it down if necessary.
2 Save Project – compare with 6.5.cpr.

Figure P6.21 Trumpet 3.

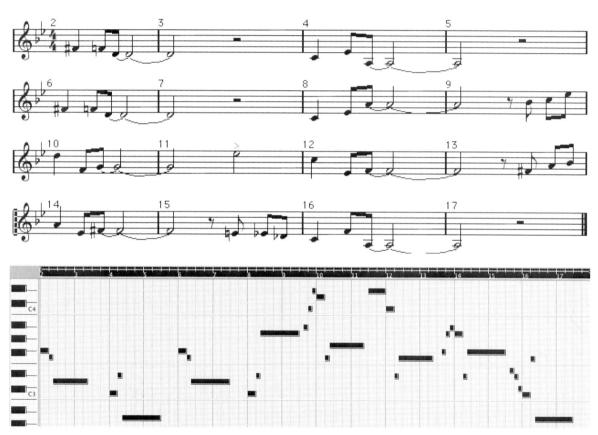

Figure P6.22 Trumpet 3, Key Editor view.

By selecting all the recorded brass parts you can examine the harmony in the Score Editor. Three-part, close voicing is used to provide a full brassy sound and for the first half of the tune, the anacrusis is left to just trumpet 1. (Anacrusis: a posh word for 'pick up' – the note(s) preceding the main part of a musical phrase.)

The kick drum is providing the 'oomph' required but a simple snare drum part will give it a lift.

Tip

As rule of thumb, in three part sectional harmony, it's a good idea to have the outside parts form a duet and move together in parallel sixths where possible.

Take 6

Track 8: Snare Drum.
Quantize Selector: 1/8 Sw-50%.
Inspector: [out: lm-7] [chn: 10] [prg: 909].
Transport panel: (L) 2.01.01 (R) 6.01.01 Activate AQ.

Follow these steps:

1 Record the Snare (Figure P6.23, P6.24 and P6.25).
2 Copy the resulting part three more times to complete 16 bars.

Figure P6.23 (right) Snare drum.

Figure P6.24 Snare drum, Key Editor view.

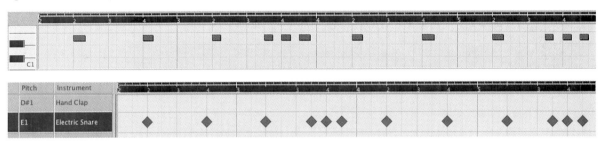

Figure P6.25 Snare drum, Drum Editor view.

The entire 16 bars will stand a repeat, but first:

1 Use the Scissors tool to make a cut between bars 1 and 2 on the trumpet 1 track, to isolate the 'pickup'.
2 Drag a copy of the new part (bar 1) and drop it on top of bar 17 to create another 'pickup'.
3 Now, using the Range tool, select everything between bars 2 – 18 and repeat once [Edit > Repeat...] (Figure P6.26a and P6.26b).
4 Save Project – compare with 6.6.cpr.

Figure P6.26a The Range tool

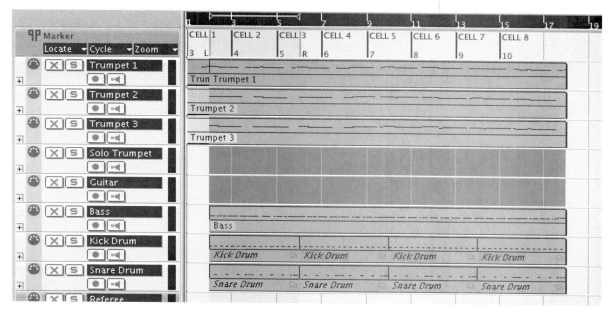

The piece is now one minute long. Time for an ending. It has to be short and snappy to fit the brief.

Figure P6.26b Selecting bars 2 – 18 with the Range tool.

Take 7

1 Set the Locators to (L) 34. 01. 01 (R) 37.01.01.
2 Record the trumpets, bass and kick drum parts in Figure P6.27 – P6.32. The brass needs to be straight here so use 1/8 – Note quantisation.
3 Save Project – compare with 6.7.cpr.

Figure P6.27 Trumpet, bass and kick drum parts.

Figures P6.28, P6.29 and P6.30 Key Editor views of Trumpet 1, Trumpet 2 and Trumpet 3.

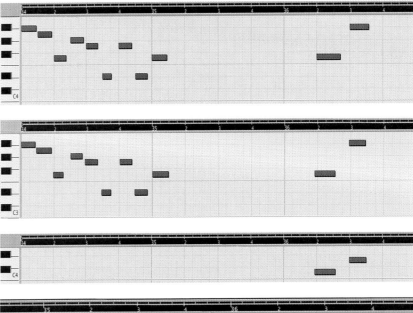

Figures P6.28, P6.29 and P6.30 Key Editor views of Trumpet 1, Trumpet 2 and Trumpet 3.

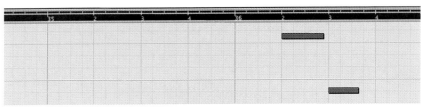

Figure P6.31 Bass, Key Editor view.

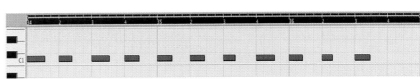

Figure P6.32 Kick drum, Key Editor view.

The repeated section from bar 18 onwards sounds fine but there's room for something else. What will provide a lift? The whole piece is dominated by brass and a touch more will not do any harm. Something very high might do the trick – Maynard Ferguson style.

Take 8

Track 4: Solo Trumpet.
Quantize Selector: 1/8 Sw-50%.
Inspector: [out: GM] [chn: 4] [prg: 62].
Track Parameters: Transpose 12.
Transport panel: (L) 18.01.01 (R) 37.01.01 Activate AQ.

Follow these steps:

1 Record the solo trumpet part (Figures P6.33 and P6.34). Break it down into four bar chunks if need be. Enter a transposition value of 12 in the Track Parameters. The notes in Figure P6.33 are written one octave lower than they sound.
2 Save Project – compare with 6.8.cpr.

Figure P6.33 Solo trumpet.

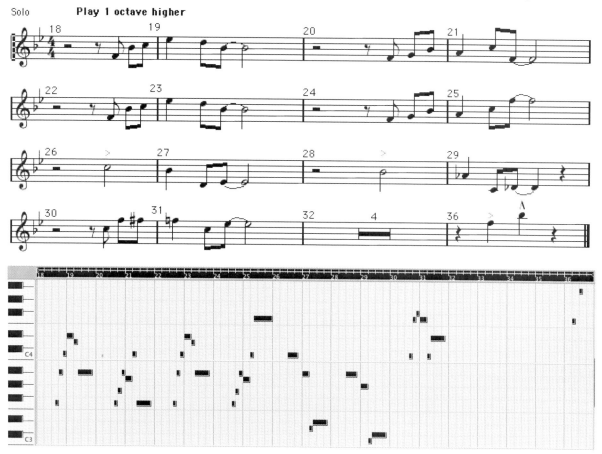

Figure P6.34 Solo trumpet, Key Editor view.

Up to now the harmony has been left to the brass. On reflection, I think the piece may now benefit from some rhythm guitar. Something sparse and choppy.

Take 9

Track 5: Guitar.
Quantize Selector: 1/8 Note.
Inspector: [out: GM] [chn: 5] [prg: 30].
Transport panel: (L) 2.01.01 (R) 18.01.01 Activate AQ.

Figure P6.35 MIDI plug-in, Compress.

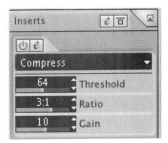

Guitar parts are usually written an octave higher than they sound, even on a Concert score. In this case, as you are probably playing a keyboard and giving a general impression of what a guitar might do here, it has been left at concert pitch. Play exactly as written. Now I don't know about you, but I tend to play rather hard when bashing out chords, guitar style, on a keyboard. This is why I've inserted the MIDI plug-in, Compress (Figure 6.35). Unless you're a rather more gentle soul, you may have to do the same! I also broke it down into four bar sections. For a looser sound apply Iterative Quantize.

Follow these steps:

1 Record the guitar part (Figures P6.36 and P6.37).
2 Save Project – compare with 6.9.cpr.

Figure P6.36 Guitar.

Figure P6.37 Guitar, Key Editor view.

3 Select the newly recorded guitar part(s) (bars 2 – 18) and repeat them between bars 18 and 34 using Edit > Repeat ... (x1).
Now for the coupe de grace!

Take 10

Track 10: Referee.
Quantize Selector: 1/16 Note.
Inspector: [out: GM] [chn: 10] [prg: Off].
Transport panel: (L) 35.01.01 (R) 37.01.01 Activate AQ.

Follow these steps:

1 Record the whistle (Figure P6.38 and P6.39), using note B3 on the keyboard.
2 Save Project – compare with 6.10.cpr.

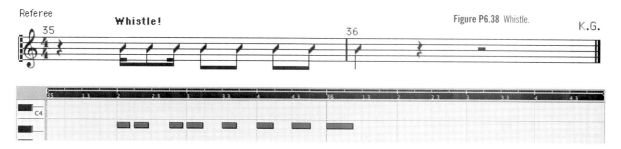

Figure P6.38 Whistle.

Figure P6.39 Whistle, Key Editor view.

Take 11 Recording an audio track

OK, apart from the mixing you're finished. Or are you? Now I'm a saxophone player and although I was happy enough with the solo trumpet part on my version, I could mentally hear a tenor sax answering those brass phrases. So I recorded an audio track.

Obviously, every reader can't follow me step by step as with the MIDI side of things (unless they happen to play tenor sax), but I can explain the process. This will serve as a guide to the general principles involved in recording vocal tracks and acoustic instruments.

Before proceeding further, I would advise readers – if they have not yet done so – to thoroughly read their manuals for a complete understanding of how Cubase SX/SL handles the audio recording process. On the surface, in the Project window, audio parts look the same as MIDI parts and are manipulated in a similar fashion. However, behind the scenes, in the editors, things are somewhat different.

OK, here's how it's done. Recording a saxophone is not so different to recording vocals. I'm using a good quality condenser mic, in preference to a dynamic type and routing the signal through an external mixing console to my sound card. To record the audio track:

1 In the Project Setup [Project > Project Setup...], decided upon a Sample Rate, Record Format and File Type to suit my particular audio hardware (Figure P6.40). Yours will of course, most likely be different.

Figure P6.40 Project Setup.

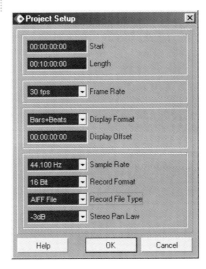

2   Ensured my audio inputs were active [Devices > VST Inputs] (Figure P6.41).

Figure P6.41 VST Input window.

3   Selected track 10: Sax.
4   Ensured the Stereo Switch was set to mono (Figure P6.42a and P6.42b).

Figure P6.42 Stereo Switch, off (mono).

5   In the Input Routing box, selected IN1 (Figure P6.43). My audio signal was entering on the left input of my stereo card as a mono signal.

Figure P6.43 Input Routing box.

6   Clicked on the Record Enable button in the Track list (Figure P6.44). The button turned red indicating record ready mode.

Figure P6.44 Record enabling a track.

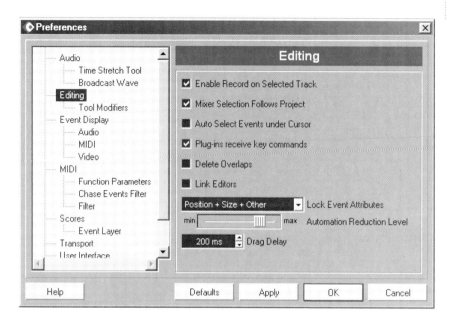

Figure P6.45 Preferences, Editing page.

Tip

If the 'Enable Record on Selected Track' is activated in the Preferences (Editing page) dialogue, tracks are automatically enabled when you select them (Figure P6.45).

7 In the Inspector, opened the Folder named Channel. This revealed a duplicate view of the Mixer Channel strip for this track (Figure P6.46).

Figure P6.46 Channel strip.

Tip

When recording audio tracks, particularly on your own, you may not want to clutter the screen with the Mixer views. In that case, use the individual Channel view for the track [Inspector > Channel folder] (Figure P6.46).

At this point I began playing the saxophone. Partly to warm up! – and partly to check the input level. This was adjusted using the output fader on my external mixer until a satisfactory level was achieved in the Track Mixer.

Info

When setting input levels, it's important to remember that the meters show the level at the input selected for the audio channel. This level can be adjusted in one of the following ways:

- By adjusting the output level of the sound source or external mixer.
- By using the audio hardware's own software mixer to set the input levels, if this is provided.
- By using the ASIO Control Panel function, if your audio hardware supports it [Device > Device Setup...]. Click the Control Panel button on the Setup tab for the VST Multitrack device.

Important note – the Channel strip faders in the Mixer are not used to alter the input level, only the recorded signal, on playback.

Everybody finds their own way of doing things. It's possible to cycle record several takes and either choose the best or edit them. The document 'Recording audio in cycle mode' in the 'Operations Manual – page 34 – explains how to do this [Help > Documentation (Acrobat PDF format > Operation Manual]. I prefer to record a 'take' and listen back. If I like it – great. If I don't, I delete it and record another straight away. In Cubase SX/SL this 'take' – referred to as an audio event – is not actually deleted, but remains on the hard disk, in the Pool's Trash folder, so I can change my mind and recall it later.

Audio files, clips and events

When audio is recorded in Cubase SX/SL three things happen:

1 An 'audio file' is created on the computer's hard disk.
2 An 'audio clip' is also created in the Pool. This 'audio clip' is a direct reference to the 'audio file' itself.
3 An 'audio event' is created on the selected audio track, in the Project window. This 'audio event' plays back the audio clip.

Playing the saxophone and recording – pressing record buttons on and off at the same time etc. – is an unwieldy, and potentially dangerous task to say the least. Fortunately the whole process can be automated in Cubase SX/SL (not the sax playing of course!) Before recording the sax, I:

1 Muted the solo trumpet on Track 4.
2 Set the Locators at (L) 18. 1. 1 (R) 26. 1. 1
3 Activated both the Punch In and Punch Out buttons on the Transport panel (Figure P6.47).
4 Scrolled back a few bars and pressed Play. When the Project cursor reached bar 18, on came the red light and Cubase SX/SL entered record mode. I blasted away on the tenor sax for eight bars, and when bar 26 arrived, off went the red light, and back on the stand went the tenor sax. A brand new audio event had appeared on the audio track.

After listening back I decided that I could do better. I could slice it up and drop in and out at various points but in my experience it's better to get things down in one take. So, I deleted the audio event (remember this is non-destructive, it's still in the Pool Trash can) and repeated the recording process. This time I'm happy. I can live with that.

Again, I knew what I wanted between bars 26 and 30, and I knew it wasn't easy, which is why I didn't include it in the first take! A very high altissimo C (concert Bb) may well need a few attempts. It did! After a satisfactory take I moved on to the

---

Tip

Audio signal input levels should be as high as possible, but to avoid distortion, make sure they do not exceed 0.0dB.

Figure P6.47 Punch In and Out buttons.

Tip

Emptying the Trash in the Pool can be done quickly, from the menu in the Project window [Pool > Empty Trash].

last four measures. Easy by comparison. One take was all that was necessary. I now had three events with corresponding audio clips in the Pool (Figure 6.48). After playing back the whole piece, I decided to keep them all.

Figure 6.48 Audio clips.

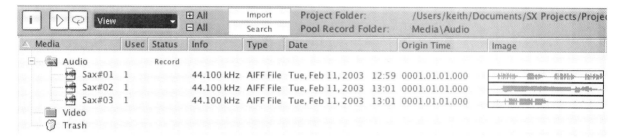

Now, I don't have unlimited hard disk space, (and neither, I expect, do you) so I emptied the Trash can in the Pool. I only wanted to keep the three good takes.

5 Save Project – compare with 6.11.cpr.

The mix

I kept things simple here and a summary is all that is necessary.

- Bass and drums are in the centre.
- Trumpet 1 is in the centre because it carries the tune.
- Trumpets 2 and 3 are supporting parts and are set at lower levels than trumpet 1. However they are panned left and right to provide a stereo spread.
- Solo trumpet is in the centre, but not too loud (muted if the sax is used).
- Guitar is placed left and kept low in the mix.
- Reverb B has been used as a Send effect. on the sax track (Figures P6. 49a and P6.49b). To use this, I first set it up as a Send Effect [Devices > VST Send Effects] by adding it to the VST Send Effect rack (Figure P6.50).

Figure P6.49a
Reverb B, send effect on sax track

Figure P6.49b Reverb B.

Figure P6.50 VST Send Effects.

Info

When using Reverb A or B as a send effect, the dry/wet mix fader can be left at 100% because you can control the balance with the send.

View and listen to the results in 6mix.cpr, muting Track 4 (MIDI – solo trumpet) and Track 10 (Audio – tenor sax) to compare versions. Now experiment with different levels and maybe inserting new send effects.

Create illusions – a big band radio jingle

J ack has a small studio set-up and runs Cubase SX/SL software. Some local jingle work has been coming his way recently and a client calls to say that he needs some big band swing music, 1940s style. He really liked the Vangelis 1980s style synth music Jack supplied for the last job, but this is a bit different. A jazz big band is comprised of seventeen instruments for a start and some pretty smart arranging techniques are needed. He decides to take on the challenge, confident that he can handle the sequencing. A friend, fresh from music college, agrees to score the 30 seconds of music required.

A day or so later his mate arrives clutching a 'hot' score for five saxes, four trumpets, four trombones and rhythm section but they soon realise that no matter how skilfully things are sequenced using sampled sounds, the end result will not be convincing enough.

It's always a little tricky to sequence acoustic instruments, even with the very best sampled instrument sounds available, but the problem seems to compound itself when a large ensemble is needed such as a symphony orchestra. Brass bands are particularly difficult, due mainly to the fact that all the instruments are using the same type of sample. As the layers are piled on a kind of MIDI soup develops. The problem is not quite so bad with a jazz big band, but care must be taken to avoid too thick a texture.

Back to Jack's problem. What's the solution? Well, he could book a large studio or a local hall and hire seventeen musicians but in Jack's case, that's the route to bankruptcy. He has another idea. Apart from being a dab hand at arranging, his pal also plays a mean saxophone. Jack decides to create an illusion.

Info

To examine the Cubase files for this chapter, copy the folder named 'big band' from the CD to your computer.

Audio and MIDI tracks combined

Once a large collection of MIDI instruments are combined as an ensemble it soon becomes obvious, even to the untrained ear, that synthesised sounds are being used. In Jack's case hiring seventeen musicians is out of the question so he decides to ask his friend to replace the virtual saxophone section with the real thing. Five saxes are used in the score, two altos, two tenors and one baritone. He doesn't own a baritone so they decide to leave that as it is.

Open bigband/jitter.cpr (Figure 8.1). Entitled *Jitterbug Jump* this is a 29 second 'sting' composed in a 1940s big band swing style and originally intended for use as library music. It's very similar to Jack's tune! This version has in fact been heavily edited from around five minutes to 30 seconds to achieve a punchy fast

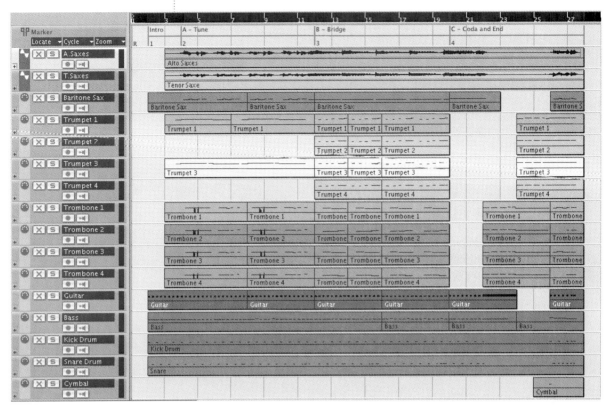

Figure 8.1 jitter.cpr.

moving sound track suitable for the role of background music to a radio jingle or similar use. This editing requires a great deal of savagery on the part of the composer. It's no good being precious about one's art in a commercial world. Things have to go. In this case it was four and a half minutes of music including a tenor saxophone jazz chorus. The Marker track indicates the construction.

- Intro – this was reduced from four bars to two.
- A – the main tune, carried by trumpets, backed by saxes and wailing trombones and reduced from 16 bars to eight.
- B – the bridge, eight bars long and carried by saxophones survives intact
- C – a huge cut to a coda and ending.

By moving quickly from one section to another within a thirty second framework the listener's attention is kept throughout. Of course it all gets shoved in the background behind somebody talking anyway, and that's another reason not get too intense about cutting things out.

The first track contains two alto saxophones and the second, two tenor saxophones. You may be wondering if I used two players on each track. I did not. Neither did I play two saxophones at once! *Jitterbug Jump* was originally recorded on a 16 track analogue tape machine and each saxophone had its own track. To save unnecessary overload on my machine's CPU (and yours) I doubled them up whilst transferring them across to Cubase.

It's worth taking a closer look at *Jitterbug Jump* because many of the topics and principles discussed in this book so far are used here.

The saxophone section

Just as a magician distracts our attention away from what he does not wish us to see, the same technique is used here. By keeping the saxophone section fairly prominent (but never dominant) our attention is focused on these 'real' instruments rather than the artificial ones. Even the fifth member of the section – the sampled baritone sax – is not really noticeable as such. There is a fair bit of unison doubling throughout and had this been a MIDI saxophone section, much pruning would have been needed to 'thin' the texture at those points. With real saxes it doesn't matter. The more the merrier.

The trumpet section

Only the lead trumpet has been assigned to the GM pre-set 'Trumpet' (Prg. 57) This sets it apart from trumpets 2, 3 and 4 which use the 'Brass Section' pre-set (Prg. 62) Where unison doubling occurs, care has been taken to avoid using the same GM voice. For example, in the opening bars, only trumpet 1 and 3 are playing. If trumpets 2 and 4 were added, MIDI soup would result. However, if this were a real brass trumpet section all four trumpets would be playing in unison here.

The trombone section

Trombones 1 and 2 have been assigned to the GM pre-set 'Trombone' (Prg. 57) and trombones 3 and 4 to the 'Brass Section' pre-set. (Prg. 62) As with the trumpets, although unison doubling does occur it only happens on separate pre-sets to avoid unnecessary thickening of the texture.

Pitch bend

Pitch bend was used between bars 2 and 11 to create the slurs. Viewed in the Score Editor, the notes are displayed at a constant pitch. Use either the Key or List Editors to view the pitch bend data.

The rhythm section

Piano has been omitted. In a real big band it would very likely be used. However the acoustic guitar provides all the rhythm and harmony needed here along with acoustic bass. Guitar chord voicing is mostly open and restricted, in the main, to four notes.

The drums

The drums have been split over three tracks. In this kind of music a real drummer may well play his snare drum on all four beats in a bar and accent the second and fourth. However, much the same effect is achieved here by omitting the first and third beats.

The mix

The instruments are panned roughly as a big-band would be seated. The only exception being bass and drums which are placed in the centre for balance. Modest amounts of reverb have been added to MIDI instruments and the saxophones are treated with a small dose of Reverb A. Any more would have created too much of a distancing effect.

Project 7: a TV sitcom theme

Musical objectives

- To construct a melody using only the notes of a blues scale.
- Fill in the harmonic and rhythmic background with the sounds of a blues band.

Cubase SX/SL skills

- Re-recording MIDI tracks as audio tracks ready for further processing and mixing.
- Inserting and utilising the built in plug-in, Rotary.
- Utilising the Reverb A plug-in as a send effect.
- Recording automation data.
- Viewing and editing Automation tracks.
- Discovering a Virtual Guitarist!

Preparation

1 From the CD, copy the folder named 'project 7' to your desktop.
2 Inside the 'project 7' folder you'll find a file named 'template7.cpr.' Open it and use it for this project.
3 Create a folder in which to save your own files as you work through the project.

The assignment

You've been commissioned to write a theme tune for a television sitcom. The main characters are two young, likeable 'no-hopers'. You know the kind of thing. They can't get the girls, they can't keep their jobs, and at the end of every episode, despite temporary success, are back where they started. The music required is to be fairly upbeat (it is a comedy) but at the same time, bluesy. Length: just under one minute. The producer is keen on tenor sax and if possible, would like it featured.

This is a tough one. How can it be kept lively and at the same time bluesy? An upbeat 12 bar blues maybe. The problem with '12 bars' is that it is hard to find a distinctive melody to fit the rather played out chord sequences. In my experience it is always a good idea to work on the melody first and harmony second. So how do you compose an instrumental blues melody line? Well the blues scale is a good starting point.

When stuck for ideas whilst writing melodies it sometimes helps to limit oneself to just a few notes. A pentatonic scale for example will provide a set of notes suitable for something rustic and folksy. In our case the blues scale, which contains one more note than a pentatonic scale, is just the job.

A pentatonic tune in the key of C will consist of the following notes: C D E G A.

OK, which key? Well tenor sax was mentioned in the brief. The key of Bb/Gm is a good key for tenor and actually puts the player in the nice easy key of C/Am. So the blues scale for this key is G Bb C C# D F G. 'That's all very well,' I can hear you say, 'the blues scale is fine for improvisation but surely it is too limiting for composing a theme tune.' Well, it's surprising just how much can be done with those six notes particularly if more than one blues scale is used. For this tune you are also going to use the C blues scale, C Eb F F# G Bb C and the D blues scale, D F G G# A C D. Now construct a tune.

So, music for the tenor saxophone is notated a tone higher than it actually sounds. Now this is sometimes convenient for the player and reduces the number of flats he would have to play if his instrument was pitched in C. The key of Ab, concert pitch, (four flats) puts him in Bb (two flats) for instance. However, it is not so good for him in sharp keys. For example, the key of C, concert pitch, will put him in the key of D containing two sharps. The key of E (four sharps) puts him in F# (six sharps).

Other common transposing instruments are:

- In Bb: trumpet, clarinet, soprano sax
- In Eb: alto sax, baritone sax
- In F: cor anglais, French horn

Some instruments, such as the piccolo and guitar, sound one octave higher than they are notated on the staff. Others such as the double bass and bass guitar sound one octave lower than written.

To gain an overall picture, at this point you may prefer to listen to the finished thing rather than just let things unfold. To do so, load 7.mix.cpr.

Info

A pentatonic scale consists of just five notes and is found in a huge amount of folk music around the world as far ranging as China, Africa and Scotland. Auld Lang Syne, for example, uses only the notes of the pentatonic scale.

Tip

It's possible to invent simple tunes very quickly using the pentatonic scale on the piano. How? – by using only the black notes starting with F#.

Info

A blues scale has only one more note than the pentatonic scale, but what a difference it makes! It's used frequently by jazz and rock soloists alike. In the key of C it will consist of: C D Eb E G A. but is usually played beginning on A, like this: A C D Eb E G A and referred to as the A blues scale.

Tip

The template has a time signature of 4/4 and the tempo is 105 bpm. Now this may be a bit fast for you. If so scroll the tempo to suit you. When listening back, scroll back to 105 bpm.

Take 1

Track 1: Melody.
Quantize Selector: 1/8 Note T.
Inspector: [out: GM] [chn: 1] [prg: 1] Grand Piano.
Transport panel: (L) 1.01.01 (R) 15.01.01 Activate AQ.

Because a blues shuffle feel is required here the Quantize Selector has been set to 1/8 Note T. The melody will eventually be played on tenor sax but for now, construct it first using a piano pre-set.

To help you decide how to break it down here's a brief analysis of the melody (Figure P7.1).

Figure P7.1 The melody.

- Bar 1 poses a musical question, bar 2 answers it. Bars 1 to 3 then, is a phrase and uses all six notes of the G blues scale.
- The phrase is repeated between bars 3 and 5 but – for variation and continuation – the last note has been changed from Bb to G.
- Bars 5 – 7 are a repetition of the first phrase but this time uses the C blues scale. It's repeated between bars 7 and 9 with pitch variation on the last two beats.
- Bars 9 – 11 are an exact repetition of the first phrase using the G blues scale.
- Bar 11 uses the D blues scale. Bar 12 is a repetition but uses the C blues scale.
- Bar 13 is an exact repetition of bar 1. Bar 14 is a new ending phrase using part of the G blues scale.

Follow these steps:

1 Record the melody in Figure P7.1. How you do it is up to you. If you are an accomplished keyboard player it can be done in one pass. It's more likely that you will opt to record it in sections (Figure P7.2, P7.3, and P7.4).

2 Save Project – compare with 7 1.cpr.

Figures P7.2, P7.3 and P7.4 Key Editor views of the melody, first, second and third sections.

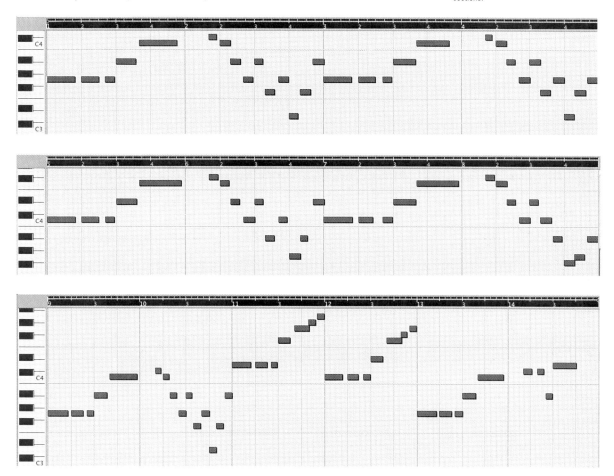

That's a chunk of the tune finished. The backing suggests itself.

Take 2

Track 2: Bass.
Quantize Selector: 1/8 Note T.
Inspector: [out: VB-1] [chn: 2] [prg: Basic Bass].
Track Parameters: Transpose -12.
Transport panel: (L) 1.01.01 (R) 15.01.01 Activate AQ.

Follow these steps:

For the bass a nice simple eighth note shuffle on the root note of each blues scale is really all that's needed. You can of course improvise on this, as would a real player. Keeping it simple though, for now at least, will help establish a clear harmonic structure.

1 Record the bass (Figure P7.5). (Note the transposition, -12). Even though the notes are written straight, play them with a triplet feel. Record it in sections maybe (Figures P7.6 and P7.7). Again how you break it down is up to you. It's not too difficult to play in one pass, except maybe for the last bar, which can be done separately. Have a go!

2 Save Project – compare with 7.2.cpr.

Figures P7.5, P7.6 and P7.7 Bass part and Key Editor views of first and second sections.

Take 3

Tracks 5, 6 and 7: Kick Drum, Snare Drum and Crash Cymbal.
Quantize Selector: 1/8 Note T.
Inspector: [out: lm-7] [chn: 10] [prg: Compressor] .
Transport panel: (L) 1. 01. 01 (R) 14. 01 01 Activate AQ.

Again simplicity is the key to a solid track here so, in a shuffle style:

1 On track 5, record the kick drum (C1) (Figures P7.8, P7.9).
2 On track 6, record the snare drum (D1) (Figures P7.10, P7.11).
3 Record the snare drum fill (L) 14. 01. 01 (R) 15. 01. 01 (Figures P7.12, P7.13).
4 On track 7, record the crash cymbal (C#2) on the first beat of bars 1, 5, and 9.
5 Save Project – compare with 7.3.cpr.

Kick Drum

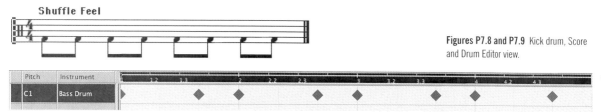

Figures P7.8 and P7.9 Kick drum, Score and Drum Editor view.

Snare Drum

Figures P7.10 and P7.11 Snare drum, Score and Drum Editor view.

Snare Drum

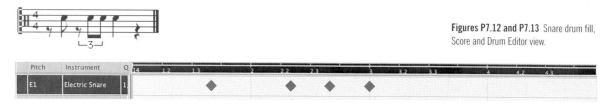

Figures P7.12 and P7.13 Snare drum fill, Score and Drum Editor view.

It's coming along isn't it? Play it through and try to imagine the two characters, maybe in a dole queue or being rebuffed by two pretty girls. What next? Well you have the basics of a blues band. Why not add guitar and organ to complete the line up?

Take 4

Track 3: Guitar.
Quantize Selector: 1/8 Note T.
Inspector: [out: GM] [chn: 3] [prg: 31] Distortion Guitar.
Transport panel: (L) 1. 01. 01 (R) 15. 01 01 Activate AQ.

Guitar parts are usually written an octave higher than they sound, even on a Concert score. In this case, as you are probably playing a keyboard, it has been left at concert pitch. Play exactly as written.

1 Record the guitar (Figure P7.14). You may well have to break it down into sections (Figures P7.15 and P7.16). Again it's a simple shuffle. A real guitar player would undoubtedly do more. However this creates the mood perfectly well.

Figure P7.14 Guitar.

2 Save Project – compare with 7.4.cpr

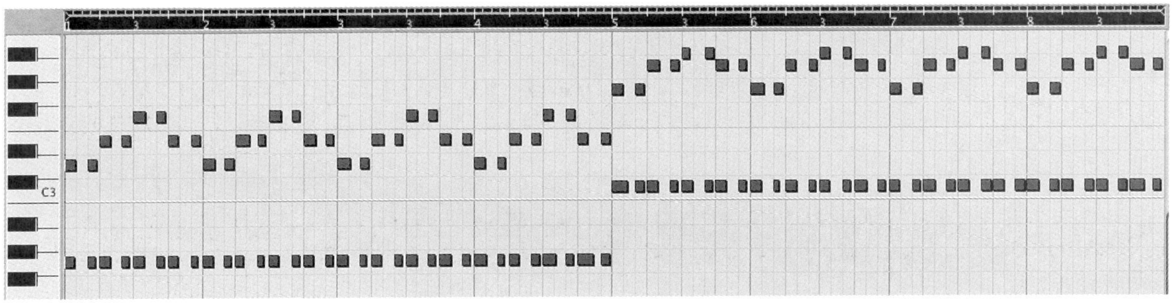

Figure P7.15 Guitar, first section, Key Editor view.

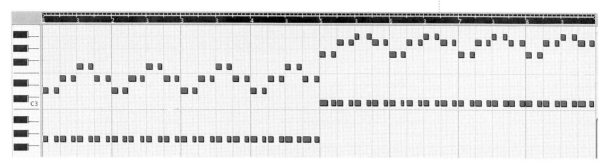

Take 5

Figure P7.16 Guitar, second section.

Track 3: Organ.
Quantize Selector: 1/8 Note T.
Inspector: [out: GM] [chn: 4] [prg: 19] Rock Organ.
Track Parameters: Transpose +12
Transport panel: (L) 1. 01. 01 (R) 15. 01 01 Activate AQ.

To repeat the shuffle pattern again would be too much of a good thing. So what to play? Something a little more spaced out is called for that does not interfere with the melody. How about this:

1 Record the organ (Figure P7.17). It sounds good one octave higher than written so use the transpose feature in the Instrument Parameters box (+12). Again, do it in sections if your keyboard skills are not too hot (Figures P7.18 and P7.19).

2 Save Project – compare with 7.5.cpr.

Figure P7.17 Organ.

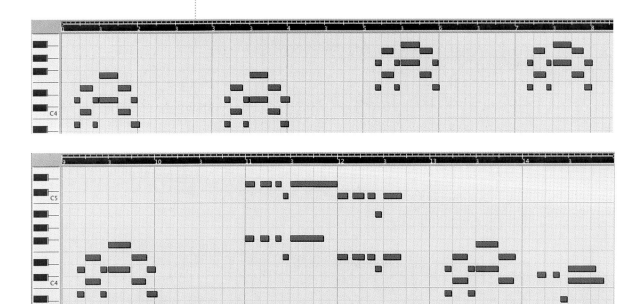

Figures P7.18 and P7.19 Organ, first and second sections, Key Editor view.

Nothing more is needed except for the tenor sax, to replace the piano. Nothing more in the way of instruments that is. There are only about 30 seconds of music so far and the assignment requires around one minute's worth. How do you extend it? Well, you could repeat it again. It might work but boredom will almost certainly creep in. No, something new is needed.

Think back to the brief. It's a comedy, but there's something a little sad about those characters. A slight change of mood could be established. But how do you do that without losing the feel? Continue to use the blues scale of course, to provide unity. Back to the piano track and melody crafting.

Take 6

1 Return to the piano track and set the locators to (L) 15. 01. 01 (R) 17. 01. 01 and record Figures P7.20 and P7.21. This phrase uses the notes of the D blues scale and takes the tune up and away from what came before. It does not need to go higher so just repeat it in a descending pattern.

2 Repeat the part twice as far as measure 21. There are now have three parts containing the same phrase.

3 Select the second part (bars 17 – 19) and use the Transpose feature [MIDI > Transpose...] to transpose it down a tone (-2) to use a C blues scale.

4 Select the third part (bars 19 – 21) and in the same way, transpose it down a fifth (-7) to use a G blues scale.

5 Set the locators to (L) 21. 01. 01 (R) 23. 1. 1 and record more piano Figure P7.22 and P7.23). This takes things nicely back home to G, so:

6 Set the locators to (L) 23. 01. 01 (R) 25. 01. 01 and record still more piano Figure P7.24 and P7.25) to finish off at about fifty-five seconds. Luv'ly job!

7 Save Project – compare with 7.6.cpr.

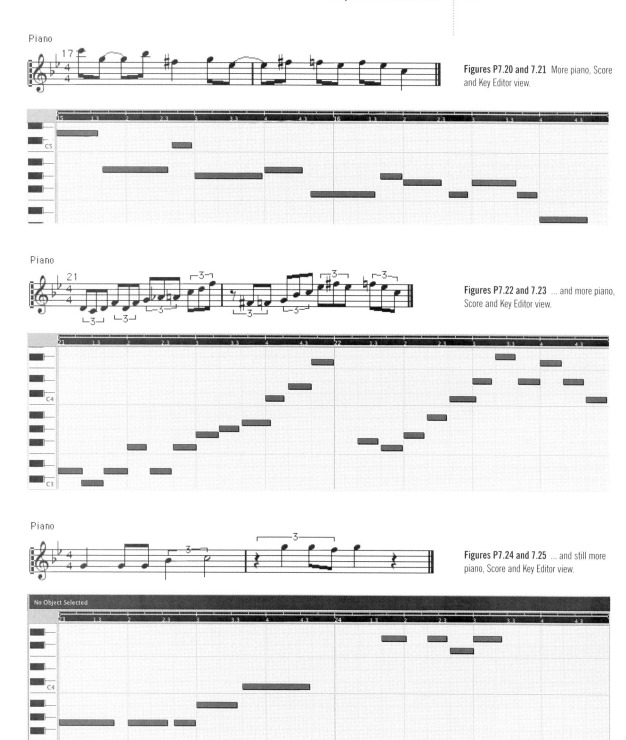

Figures P7.20 and 7.21 More piano, Score and Key Editor view.

Figures P7.22 and 7.23 … and more piano, Score and Key Editor view.

Figures P7.24 and 7.25 … and still more piano, Score and Key Editor view.

Take 7

1 Return to the bass track. In order to change the mood:
2 Set the locators to (L) 15. 01. 01 (R) 25. 01. 01 and record more bass. Do it in sections if you prefer (P7.26 and P7.27).
3 Save Project – compare with 7.7.cpr.

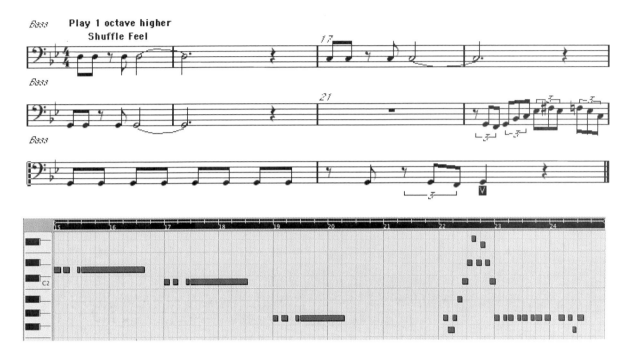

Figures P7.26 and P7.27 More bass, Score and Key Editor view.

Take 8

1 Return to the organ track.
2 Set the locators to (L) 15. 01. 01 (R) 25. 01. 01 and record more organ. Do it in sections if you prefer (Figures P7.28 and P7.29).
3 Save Project – compare with 7.8.cpr.

Figure P7.28 More organ.

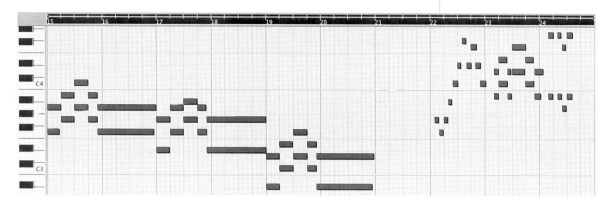

Take 9

1 Return to the guitar track.

How do you fit the distorted guitar into this more melancholic section? The most obvious answer is to leave it out. Not only would it spoil the mood, omitting it creates a nice sense of emptiness. However it will boost the unison line in bar 22, so:

2 Set the locators to (L) 22. 01. 01 (R) 25. 01. 01 and record the ending (Figures P7.30 and P7.31).

3 Save Project – compare with project 7.9.cpr.

Figure P7.29 More organ, section one, Key Editor view.

Figure P7.30 More guitar.

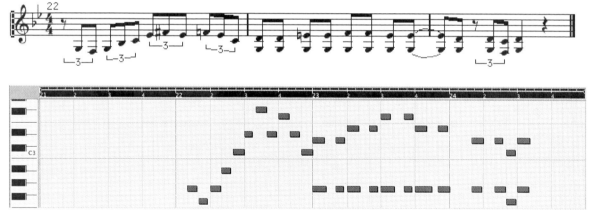

Figure P7.31 More guitar, Key Editor view.

Take 10

1 Return to the kick drum track . Set the locators to (L) 23. 01. 01 (R) 25. 01. 01 and record the ending (Figure P7.32 and P7.33).

2 Return to the snare drum track. Set the locators to (L) 22. 01. 01 (R) 25. 01. 01 and record the ending (Figure P7.34 and P7.35).

3 Save Project – compare with 7.10.cpr.

Figures P7.32 and P7.33 More kick drum, Score and Drum Editor view.

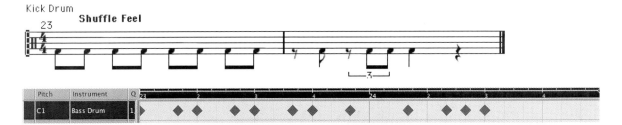

Figures P7.34 and P7.35 More snare drum, Score and Drum Editor view.

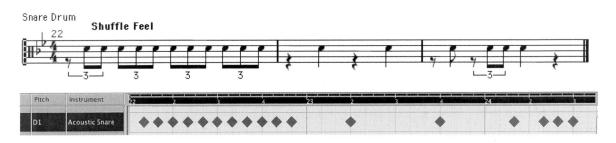

That's it. You're done. All that's needed is the tenor sax. This was recorded in one take using an external mixer and a condenser microphone. EQ was not used. For information on how to record vocals and acoustic instruments into Cubase SX/SL see Chapter 7, Audio Recording: The Basics. For a more detailed account see Project 6, Recording an Audio Track.

The mix

Open 7.mix.cpr to hear and view the tenor sax track which replaces the piano melody. A quick glance will reveal six additional audio tracks. For better mixing control, the MIDI tracks have been recorded as audio tracks. The main advantages of this? Well, once recorded as audio files they can be treated with inserts and send effects in the Track Mixer. How's it done? Route the audio output from your MIDI device to the input you use for recording audio into Cubase SX/SL. Exactly how this is achieved will depend on your particular hardware set-up. Likely sources will be either a sound module, synthesiser, sound card or external mixer. You may even have a sound card that includes an option to route the signal internally. Once the signal reaches Cubase SX/SL, just record the audio as you would any other audio source.

Tip

When mixing, MIDI tracks can be re-recorded as audio tracks. How? – route the MIDI output (audio) to the audio input used to record into Cubase SX/SL.

OK, now examine 7.mix. in the Mixer.

- Reverb A has been set up as a send effect and is used on the tenor sax, organ and guitar tracks. The Medium pre-set is is used.
- Rotary has been inserted on the organ track (Figure P7.36). The Dirty Les pre-set was used and does a decent job of emulating a Leslie cabinet . Wonderful sounding things, coupled with a Hammond organ, but not much fun to carry down the stairs to a basement club gig, believe me.

For flexibility, when re-recording MIDI tracks as audio, record each MIDI part as a separate audio file, including individual drum sounds. To do this, use the Mute and Solo functions.

Figure P7.36 Rotary, Dirty Les pre-set.

- MIDI tracks – all seven are muted now because they have been re-recorded as audio tracks.
- The tenor sax remains in the centre of the mix, and because it carries the tune, is treated to just a little more reverb than the other instruments.
- Drums are in the centre of the stereo picture and, in this case, the kick drum is left dry. A small amount of snare drum is sent to Reverb A. Because of the fairly long reverb being used, any more would sound very messy. To save processing power, only one reverb unit has been used. Feel free to add another if your computer's CPU can cope.
- The VB-1 pre-set was changed from Basic Bass to Warm Bass. Nothing further was done and it's left dead centre in the stereo picture.
- Guitar is panned left and treated with a touch of reverb. Notice anything else? On close listening you'll discover that it's a different guitar part. Not only that, it sounds like a real guitarist playing. So who's the guitarist? Well it's a guy named Thomas Blug. I didn't fly Thomas over from Germany to record the track. Instead, I used Virtual Guitarist, Electric Edition, a VST Instrument from Steinberg (Figure P7.37). I chose a rock 'n' roll shuffle pre-set from one of the many excellent rhythms available and after quickly drawing the chords in the Key Editor, left it up to the virtual Herr Blug to lay down a solid track. A great job he made of it too!

Processing more than one track with reverb set up as a send effect saves CPU power compared to inserting it directly into multiple tracks.

Figure P7.37 Virtual Guitarist, Electric Edition.

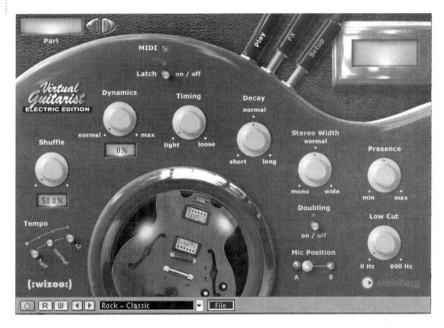

- Organ is panned right and treated with a little reverb. Another device, Cubase SX/SL's Rotary has been inserted here.
- Automation is used on the organ track. With the Mixer open, play the piece through. At bar 15, where things cool down a little, the volume fader rises a little. When the band returns in full, the volume returns to it's previous level.

Return to the Project window to view the automation data another way (Figure P7.38). Select the organ track and you will see a blue horizontal line. Follow it along and you will notice it rise a little just before bar 15. It returns to something close to the previous level just before bar 23. 'That's all very well', you say, 'but how was it done?'

Figure P7.38 Organ track – automation data.

As with most functions in Cubase SX/SL there are several ways of doing things. Automating the volume was done in the Mixer by:

1 In the Project window, on the Toolbar, ensuring Touch Fader was selected from the drop-down menu (Figure P7.39). This is the most commonly used automation mode.

Figure P7.39 Touch Fader selected.

2 Selecting the organ track and and activating the Write button (Figure P7.40).
3 Pressing play, and as the music approached bar 15, raising the volume fader a little. On reaching bar 21, returning the fader to its previous position and turning off the Write button.
4 Playing back the piece and checking the volume with the Read button activated – the faders move automatically – (Figure P7.41).

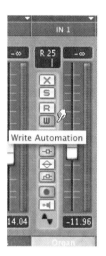
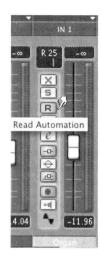

Figures P7.40 and P7.41 The Write and Read buttons.

Info

The record button on the Transport panel does not have to be activated when recording real time automation data – just play the track.

Another way to do this would be to draw the information directly onto the Automation track, in the Project window. I find using the Mixer more intuitive for recording volume changes and use the Automation track for editing. It's horses for courses.

Right, that's it. As usual, there's always another way to mix things. I'm happy, but please feel free to experiment with it further. For example, try redrawing the automation data in the Automation track with the pencil and eraser tools. I've left the EQ alone, but there's room for improvement. Cutting the lower frequencies on the guitar perhaps.

Minimalism

Minimalism, as a musical art movement began in the early 1960s and was brought to prominence by Terry Riley with his enormously influential piece entitled 'In C'. It has been growing steadily ever since and composers such as Philip Glass, Steve Reich, John Adams, and Michael Nieman, are all very successful in this genre, writing music for film and theatre as well as concert works. Indeed the music of Glass and Reich is now so frequently imitated that the style can be heard on all manner of television commercials and incidental music.

The cyclic and repetitive techniques used in minimalism often produce music of a static nature ideally suited for use with the moving image in the form of atmospheric soundtracks. These same techniques also make it ideal music for composing within sequencers such as Cubase. However because the music is essentially repetitive, many people mistakenly believe that all they have to do is compose a few measures and apply the Repeat function. This inevitably leads to very boring music indeed. To make it interesting, just as in all other forms of music, repetition must be combined with variation.

There are many techniques used in minimalism and the repetitive nature of the music often belies it's complexity. I have chosen two techniques used by minimalist composers to examine.

Follow these steps:

• Load minimal1.cpr.

Set the MIDI output to your GM sound source.

A gradual cumulative process of adding notes is used here (Figures 9.1, 9.2 and 9.3). It's a simple technique which quickly leads to very complex structures. Bar 1 contains a group of seven notes of equal length (1/8 notes) which are repeated three times in succession. In bar 5 an extra note is added to the group and another at bar 9. If these twelve bars are cycled round you hear first an expanding effect and then as the cycle begins again a contracting one. The general melodic structure remains the same whilst quite different rhythmic structures emerge.

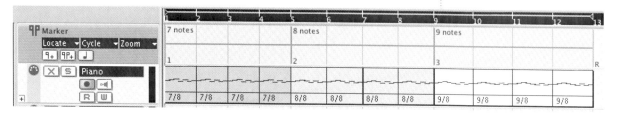

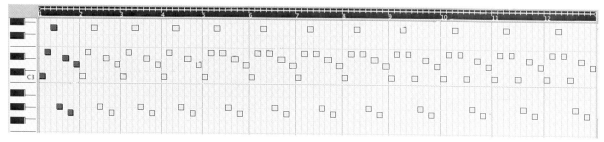

Piano

Figures 9.1 – 9.3 minimal1, Project window
view, Key Editor view and Score Editor view.

- Load minimal2.cpr.

Set the MIDI output to your GM sound source.

Repeating two or more rhythmic patterns of different lengths simultaneously is another technique. In minimal2 (Figures 9.4, 9.5 and 9.6) the first right hand piano part is two bars long and is repeated twice making a total of six bars. The left hand part however is only one and a half bars long and has to be repeated three times to finish along with the right hand part. When both parts are viewed together in the Score editor seven bars of music in 4/4 are seen. The result is rather hypnotic and although the music is repetitive no two measures are the same.

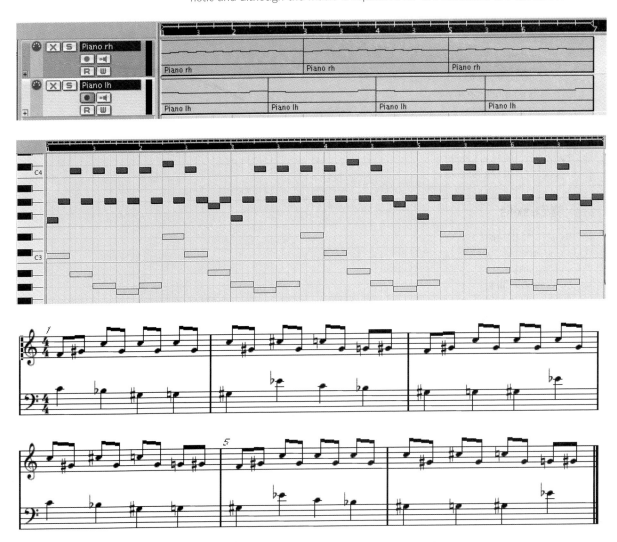

Figures 9.4 – 9.6 minimal2, Project window view, Key Editor view and Score Editor view.

In the next chapter similar techniques to those above are used and combined with pre-recorded audio parts to produce a minimalist piece of music.

Project 8: a minimalist soundtrack

Musical objectives

- Use a pentatonic scale to construct a simple ostinato, oriental in character and suitable for manipulation in a minimalist fashion.
- Decide upon instrumentation to create an atmosphere for film clip depicting an oriental landscape.
- Create 'cycles' using repetitive techniques to generate new patterns.
- Introduce new musical elements that coincide with, and enhance the addition of a procession in the landscape film.

Cubase SX/SL skills

- Inserting RPN (Registered Parameter Number) messages.
- Setting synthesiser pitch bend range.
- Renaming parts.
- Importing audio files.
- Delaying audio tracks.
- Using the Dynamics processor, Compress.
- Creating a fade-out with mix automation.

Preparation

1 From the CD, copy the folder named 'project 8' to your desktop.
2 Inside the 'project 8' folder you'll find a file named 'template8.cpr'. Open it and use it for this project.
3 Create a folder in which to save your own files as you work through the project.

The assignment

Using minimalist techniques, compose a piece of music about one and a half minutes long for use as a soundtrack with an oriental landscape scene. The scene first opens with an empty landscape. After about 20 seconds we see the beginnings of a procession of people appear on the horizon. The procession winds its way into the foreground. After about 55 seconds we can see that the procession contains not only marching figures but acrobats and elephants. After about a minute and a half, the procession has passed and gradually disappears from view.

Info

The template has a time signature of 4/4 and the tempo is 108 bpm. Now this may be a bit fast for you. If so scroll the tempo to suit. Mute the audio tracks when recording at a slower speed (they cannot be slowed with the MIDI tracks). When listening back, change the tempo to 108 bpm again.

As with previous projects, you may prefer to listen to the finished article before going further. To do this, open either 8.11.cpr or 8.mix.cpr and play it through a few times.

Take 1

Track 1: Guitar – stereo audio track.
Toolbar: Snap set to Bar.
Transport panel: (L) 1 01,01.

Follow these steps:

1 Ensure the Project Position Line is at 1.01.01, and from the project8 folder, import the audio file named guitar.aif [File > Import > Audio File...]. This is a pre-recorded audio file, containing a very simple ostinato which is repeated throughout the composition . It actually consists of an acoustic guitar and a harp sample. A stereo audio event is created (Figure P8.1).

2 On playing, you will notice the guitar begins on the first beat of the bar. Well, you need it to begin on the second eighth note of the bar so, in the Inspector, type in or use the slider to set a Delay of 278 milliseconds – one eighth note at this speed (Figure P8.2). Play it through. Checking it against the metronome click will illustrate the parameter change. Now, you need this one bar audio event to repeat continuously throughout the piece. For now, repeat it 13 times.

3 Save Project – compare with 8.1.cpr.

Figure P8.1 Audio event (stereo).

Figure P8.2 Delaying the audio event.

The Delay value is displayed as milliseconds. How then do you set a delay value corresponding to bars and beats?

1 With the Transport panel display set to Bars + Beats (Figure P8.3a), move the project cursor to the delay point (Figure P8.3b).

2 Change the display to Seconds (Figure P8.3c).

3 Use the newly displayed figure as your Delay value.

Figure 8.3a Transport panel display, Bars-Beats.

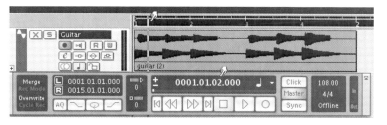

Figure 8.3b Transport panel display, delay point.

Figure 8.3c Transport panel display, seconds

Take 2

Track 2: Pizzicato Str.
Quantize Selector: 1/8 Note.
Inspector: [out GM] [chn: 1] [prg: 46] Pizzicato Strings.
Transport panel: (L) 3.01.01 (R) 5.01.01.

The brief requires something oriental in character and the most obvious thing that comes to mind is the pentatonic scale E G A B D. However the guitar is only playing two notes and it would be nice to keep things simple. So let's drop the G and the A. That leaves E, B and D with which to build another ostinato. A light texture is required. How about pizzicato strings? Violins are not oriental instruments as such, but when plucked strings are used they provide that kind of flavour.

Follow these steps:

1   Record the pizzicato strings (Figures 8.4 and P8.5). Minimalism, as we know, is about repetition. We also know that variation is needed to stimulate interest so you are now going to duplicate the part just recorded and then work on each resulting part individually.

Figure P8.4 Pizzicato strings.

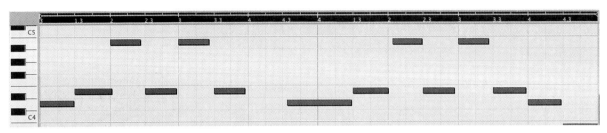

Figure P8.5 Pizzicato strings, Key Editor view.

2 Repeat the pizzicato strings (bars 3 – 5) five times as far as bar 15.

3 Now here's what you are going to do. Each part will keep it's rhythmic structure but the notes will be changed according to a few simple rules:

- The first part (bars 1 – 3) remains unaltered. We'll refer to this as the 'Original part.'
- The second part (bars 3 – 5) begins on the second note of the Original part.
- The third part (bars 5 – 7) begins on the third note of the Original part.

4 Repeat the process on the remaining parts until you have a 12 bar ostinato, named 'Cycle 1' in the Marker (Figure P8.6).

5 Save Project – compare with 8.2.cpr.

Figure P8.6 Cycle 1.

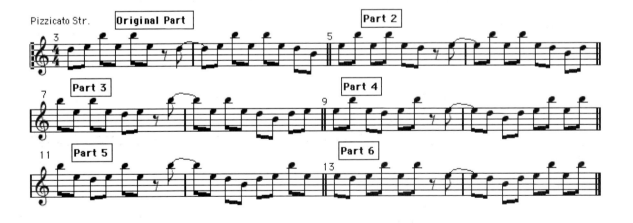

Take 3

Quantize Selector: 1/8 Note.
Inspector: [out GM] [chn: 2] [prg: 42] Viola.
Track Parameters: Transpose -12.

Follow these steps:

1 Return to the pizzicato string track and glue the pizzicato string parts together as one.
2 With Snap set to Beat, drag a copy of the pizzicato string part to 4.03.01 on the viola track. Ensure that Transpose is set to -12 in the Track Parameters. Rename the part in the Project Browser.
3 Play back the piece. The 12 bar ostinato 'Cycle 1' begins with the pizzicato strings and is echoed as a canon, one and a half bars later by the viola (Figure P8.7). Things are becoming interesting even though only three notes have so far been used. Already you have the oriental backdrop required.
4 Open the Mixer and, depending on how you played, adjust the volume levels of the pizzicato strings and the viola. Because they are both playing essentially the same thing, and to avoid confusion, pan the viola to the right and pizzicato strings to the left. Adjust the guitar track volume too.
5 Save Project – compare with 8.3.cpr.

Info

Unlike in Cubase VST parts cannot be renamed in the Project window. Instead open the Project Browser [Project > Browser] and type in new names for the parts (Figure P8.8).

Figure P8.7 Pizzicato string and viola Canon.

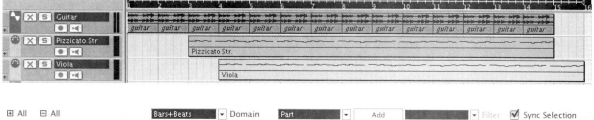

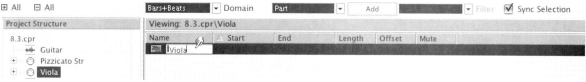

Figure P8.8 Renaming parts.

Info

A canon contains musical imitation. A melodic strand is repeated after a certain interval, in our case after one and a half bars. There are many forms of canon. The imitation may be at the octave, or another interval such as a fifth. Simple canons take the form of a round such as 'London's Burning' or 'Frere Jacques.'

Take 4

Track 4: Oboe – mono audio track.

Follow these steps:

1 Place the project cursor at 3.01.01, and from the project8 folder import the audio file named oboe.aif. This is a pre-recorded mono audio file which contains a four bar ostinato melody. Adjust the volume accordingly.
2 Select the oboe audio event and, as with the guitar audio event, repeat it as far as bar 15.
3 Save Project – compare with 8.4a.cpr.
4 Select the guitar, pizzicato strings and oboe parts (bars 3 – 15) and repeat them three times as far as bar 51.
5 Select the viola part (4.03.01 – 16.03.01) and repeat it three times as far as 52. 03. 01.
6 Save Project – compare with 8.4b.cpr.

You have reached the point where the beginning of a procession appears.

Take 5

Track 5: Strings 1.
Quantize Selector: 1/8 Note.
Inspector: [out: GM] [chn: 3] [prg: 49] Strings.
Transport panel (L): 11.01.01 (R) 17.01.01.

A glance at the strings 1 part (Figure P8.13) will reveal a glissando from D down to G. You can achieve this by just playing the note D2 and using the Pitch Bend controller on your MIDI keyboard for the slide down of seven semitones. But first you have to ensure that your GM sound source will receive the information. To do this, you will need to insert an RPN (Registered Parameter Number) message in the Event List window to define the pitch bend sensitivity.

Follow these steps:

1 Position the project cursor at bar 11, and with the Pencil tool, create a Part by clicking at bar 11 and extending it as far as bar 17.
2 With the new part selected, open the Key Editor [MIDI > Open Key Editor].
3 The Key Editor window is split horizontally into two parts, the lower being a controller lane . The drop-down menu, on the left contains a list of controllers available for use (Figure P8.9). You need the following controllers: RPN LSB, RPN MSB and DataEnt MSB. Now, it may be that these will be missing from the list. If that's the case, select Setup to gain access to the Controllers Menu Setup and add the controllers you need from the 'Hidden' section (Figure P8.10).

Tip

Double click between locators with the arrow tool to create a part – nice and quick.

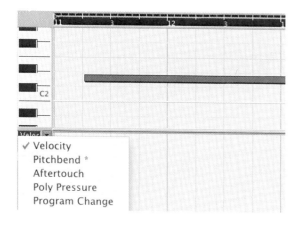

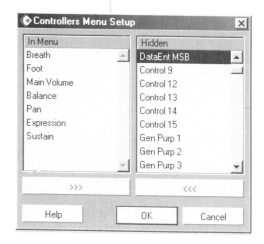

4 From the menu, select RPN MSB, ensure that Snap is active and with the Pencil tool add a controller event with a value of 0 (Figure P8.11a).

5 From the menu, select RPN LSB and add a second event, again with a value of 0 (Figure P8.11b).

6 From the menu, select DataEnt MSB and add a third event, this time with a value of seven (Figure P8.11c). Seven represents the pitch bend range.

7 Open the List Editor to view the data in more detail (Figure P8.12). Note how I have separated each event by a few ticks.

Figure P8.9 (left) The controller lane and menu.

Figure P8.10 (right) The Controllers Menu Setup.

Figures P8.11a, b and c
Controller RPN MSB (101).
Controller RPN LSB (100).
Controller DataEnt MSB (6).

L	Type	Start	End	Length	Data 1	Data 2	Channel
	Controller	0011.01.01.000			RPN MSB	0	3
	Controller	0011.01.01.004			RPN LSB	0	3
	Controller	0011.01.01.008			DataEnt MSB	7	3

Figure P8.12 Controllers, List Editor view.

If you happen to be using Steinberg's Universal Sound Module as your GM sound source, setting the pitch bend range is a simple matter. Move the slider to 7 (Figure P8.13). (The USM is hidden away in the VST 5 Instruments folder – see *How to use this book and CD* on page 1).

Figure P8.13 USM pitch bend range set to 7.

this book and CD on page 1).

Info

Part of the GM specification RPN (Registered Parameter Numbers) messages are MIDI controller numbers that allow us to change the parameters of tones such as: Pitch Bend Sensitivity, Master Fine Tuning etc. Each RPN is made up of a Controller Number and value.

Phew! That's the complicated stuff over. The General MIDI sound module will now have a pitch bend range, up or down, of seven semitones. On with the music.

1 Record the strings 1 part (Figures P8.14 and P8.15). To achieve the descending glissando from D down to G just play the note D2 and use the pitch bend controller on your MIDI keyboard for the slide down.

Another way to do it is to record or draw the note first, and add the glissando afterwards in the Key Editor controller lane with Pitch Bend selected . Snap will need to be off, to draw a nice smooth line. However, in my experience it's usually best to record it as you play. Less of a fiddle. It's also worth checking to see that Pitch Bend has been reset at the end of the note. If not the next note on that channel will sound terribly wrong! Do this in the List Editor (Figure P8.16).

2 Save Project – compare with 8.5a.cpr.

Figures P8.14 and 8.15 Strings 1, Score Editor and Key Editor view.

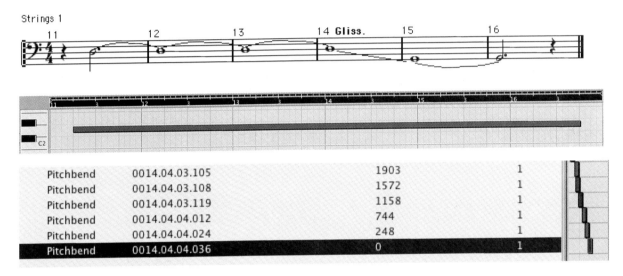

Figure P8.16 Pitch bend reset data.

The strings could be stronger. How about doubling them one octave lower? Follow these steps:

1 Select the Strings 1 part and drag a copy to track 6. Ensure that it starts at bar 11. Rename the part Strings 2 in the Project Browser.

2 In the Parameters section, transpose the new string part down an octave (-12).

3 In the Mixer adjust the volume for Strings 1 and 2. Avoid having them too loud. I panned them hard left and right for separation. The effect is more dramatic too.

4 Save Project – compare with 8.5b.

Take 6

1 Return to the Strings 1 track, set the locators at (L) 17.01.01 (R) 23.01.01 and record a second glissando in the same manner as the first. This time play C2 and glide down to F (Figures P8.17 and P8.18). Again, copy the resulting part to the Strings 2 track. Transpose it down one octave (-12). As before, rename the part in the Project Browser and check the pitch bend reset data.
2 Save Project – compare with 8.6.cpr.

Figure P8.17 More strings.

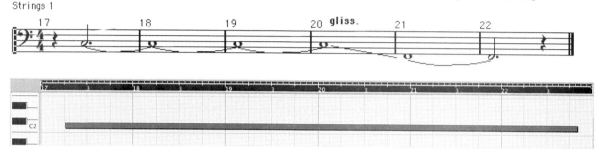

You have now reached the point where the full procession including the acrobats and animals is in view.

Figure P8.18 More strings, Key Editor view.

Take 7

1 Return to the String 1 track.
2 Set locators at (L) 27.01.01 (R) 31.01.01 and record the strings (Figure P8.19 and P8.20).
3 Copy the resulting part to the String 2 track, and rename it. You have already transposed the track so it will play an octave lower.
4 Select both the String 1 and 2 parts between bars 27 and 32 and repeat them three times as far as bar 43.
5 Save Project – compare with 8.7.cpr.

Figure P8.19 Strings.

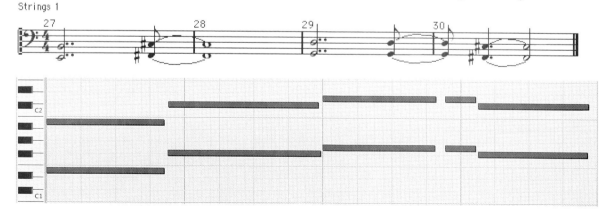

Figure P8.20 Strings, Key Editor view.

Take 8

1 Return to the String 1 track. Set the locators at (L) 43.01.01 (R) 53.01.01 and record the strings in Figures P8.21 and P8.22.

2 Copy the resulting part to the String 2 track and rename it.

3 Save Project – compare with 8.8.cpr.

Figure P8.21 More strings.

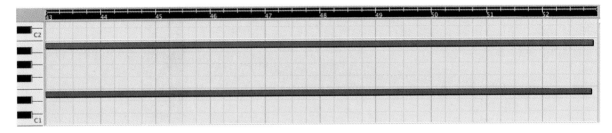

Figure P8.22 More strings, Key Editor view.

You now have strings, one octave apart, playing a moving line and creating a contrast with the repeating ostinati above. Something more is needed to add extra weight and bass and drums are the obvious choice. I think a slap bass is needed to give the edge needed to cut through those low strings.

Take 9

Track 7: Bass Guitar mono audio track.

1 Ensure the Project cursor is at 27.01.01 and from the project8 folder import the audio file bass1.aif [File > Import > Audio File...]. This is a pre-recorded audio file containing a four bar riff derived from the ostinati playing above it but also follows the harmonic progression of the string line.

2 Copy and paste the resulting audio event to bar 31, 35, and 39, making sure the copies always snap dead on the first beat of the bar.

3 Set the Project cursor to 43.01.01 and from the project8 folder import the audio file bass2.aif to complete the bass line.

4 Save Project – compare with 8.9.cpr.

All that are needed are the drums.

Take 10

Track 8: Drums.
Quantize Selector: 1/16 Note.
Inspector: [out: lm-7] [chn: 10] [prg: Compressor].
Transport panel: (L) 26. 01. 01 (R) 44. 01. 01.

1 Record the drum part (Figure P8.23). Bar 26 is an intro fill (Figure P8.24). 27
   to 43 is a two bar pattern, repeated using bass drum and snare (Figure
   P8.25). Bar 43 is a cymbal crash (Figure P8.26). It can all be played quite
   easily in one pass on a keyboard but break it down if need be. I used Iterative
   Quantize to tighten things up a bit.
2 Save Project – compare with 8.10.cpr.

Figure P8.23 Drum part.

Figure P8.24 Intro fill, Drum Editor view.

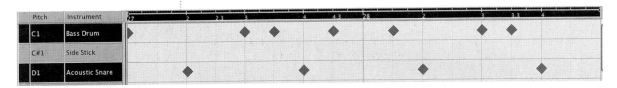

Figures P8.25 and 8.26 Drum Editor view of Two bar pattern and Cymbal crash.

Take 11

Track 9: Tambourine.
Quantize Selector: 1/8 Note.
Inspector: [out: GM] [chn: 10] [prg: off].
Transport panel: (L) 27.01.01 (R) 43.01.01.

1 The tambourine (F#2) plays a 1 bar pattern (Figure P8.27 and P8.28) repeatedly between the locators. I used Iterative Quantize to tighten things up a little.
2 Save Project – compare with 8.11.cpr.

Figures P8.27 Tambourine.

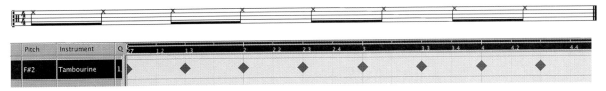

Figure P8.28 Tambourine, Key Editor view.

The final mix

A final mix can be seen and heard in 8.mix (Figure P8.29). Where have all the MIDI tracks gone? I re-recorded them as audio files and deleted them. It's not a particularly easy mix and this way allows more control by using EQ, inserts and send effects. Another reason? You can hear things exactly as they are because you are not relying on different GM tone generators. Open the Mixer, have a look around and play it through.

There's a lot going on, particularly from bar 27 onwards. The bass benefits from some compression, courtesy of Compress (Figure P8.30). Use the Bypass Inserts button on the channel strip to hear the difference (Figure P8.31). Drums too have been treated with compression. Reverb A is used as a send effect (Figure P8.32) and applied to drums – just a touch – and oboe. A long pre-set is used to 'float' the oboe above the general racket!

Figure P8.29 The final mix.

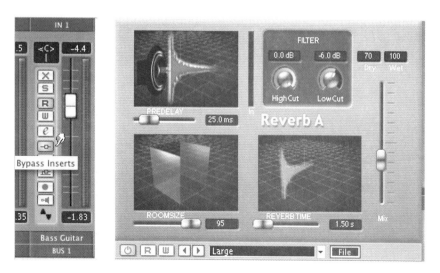

Figure P8.30 (left) Compress, used on the bass.

Figure P8.31 (below) Insert Bypass button.

Figure P8.32 (right) Send effect, Reverb A.

- The Attack control determines how soon compression kicks in above the set threshold level.
- The Release control how soon it returns to its original level.
- The MakeUp Gain control is used to compensate for the gain reduction, displayed in the Gain Reduction meter.

By now you've probably spotted those magic faders, moving all by themselves to create a fade out. This automation data can be viewed in the Project window [Project > Show Used Automation]. Nodes were inserted with the Pencil tool to create the fade. The strings are panned hard right and left. The pizzicato strings and viola also use opposite sides of the stereo spectrum.

Have a mess with it . There's some scope for EQ, although care was taken to choose instruments that did not all use the same frequency ranges. If your system can take it, try inserting more plug-ins. Go easy on the reverb though. This tune gets very messy, very quickly!

Dance music

D ance music started in the mid 1980s and nobody thought it would last. Here we are in the twenty-first century and it's still with us and getting stronger. Why is it so popular? Because people love dancing to it. More to the point, young people love dancing to it, and that's why it is being featured more and more in radio and TV commercials targeted specifically at the young. It also forms a backdrop to many sports, motoring, even wildlife programs on TV as well as frequent use in drama, soaps and films.

Styles and loops

Of course, there are many styles within this genre – House, Garage, Trance, Drum & Bass, Hip Hop and Ambient to name just a few – but when used as background music the actual style is not so important. What is important is the general impression that the product being plugged, or the program being watched, is cool and up to date! Unlike most Dance Music there is sometimes a strong melodic line and more harmonic movement involved but the key ingredient is always rhythm. Drum and bass loops being the most prominent features.

There are many excellent loops available from companies such as PocketFuel, and these can often make a good starting point. I have made use of a PocketFuel loop myself in Project 9. Trawling through hundreds of loops can be time consuming and often it is quicker to make your own, particularly if you have a specific brief to work to. This is after all, far more creative. And where's an ideal place to construct loops? Cubase SX/SL for one! Once you have made one or two, confidence grows, and before you know it you may well have a large library of your own original loops.

Constructing a drum and bass loop

Realism gives way to creativity when making loops, although it cannot be disregarded altogether. The most popular drum machines, such as the TR808 started life emulating acoustic kits, even though they are chosen for different reasons today. Bass drum, snare drum, toms and hi-hats are all present on acoustic kits and function the same way on virtual kits. The beauty of using them in Dance Music is the knowledge that they do not necessarily have to sound anything like a real drummer. We are limited only by our imagination. Having said that, control is needed. As in most creative forms, no matter how complicated, simplicity lies at the heart of things.

Here's a four-bar loop to examine.

1 Load loops/latloop.cpr.

2 Set the MIDI output to your GM sound source. and have a listen.

It's fast, frenetic and Latin in style. It doesn't belong to any particular dance music genre but would be a suitable starting point for a number of uses – a carnival scene maybe. All percussion work was done in the Drum Editor using the Drumstick tool to enter the notes with a mouse. Here's a breakdown.

- Tempo: fast, frantic, Latin – 140 bpm seemed appropriate.
- Track 1: Bass Drum (C1) – an event is placed on every beat of each bar (Figure 10.1).

Figure 10.1 Bass drum beats.

- Track 2: Pedal Hi-hat (G#1) – a beat on every other eighth-note . Placing them between the bass drum adds a sense of urgency (Figure 10.2).

Figure 10.2 Hi-hat beats.

- Track 3: Low Middle Tom (B1) – a simple back-beat pattern (Figure 10.3).

Figure 10.3 Low Middle Tom beats.

- Track 4: Electric Snare (E1) – a simple pattern between bars 1 and 3 is copied between bars 3 and 5 (Figure 10.4). It's the snare that brings this pattern alive. The Grid value was changed to 32 for the snare rolls. For realism, I drew a velocity ramp in the controller lane. (Figure 10.5)

Figure 10.4 Electric Snare beats.

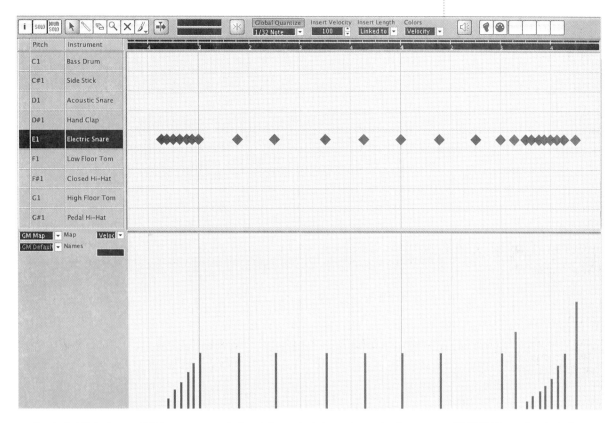

• Track 5: High Agogo (G3) – a pattern in bar 1 is copied throughout the loop (Figure 10.6).

Figure 10.5 Snare rolls and velocity ramp.

Figure 10.6 High Agogo beats.

• Track 6: Vibraslap (A#2) – a beat on the last sixteenth of bar 4. As each new cycle begins this has the effect of anticipating the first beat and adds to the urgency (Figure 10.7).

Figure 10.7 Vibraslap.

- Track 7: A meaty bass line was added. This was not entered with the mouse, but played in real time and not quantised. (Figures 10.8 and 10.9).

Figure 10.8 Bass line.

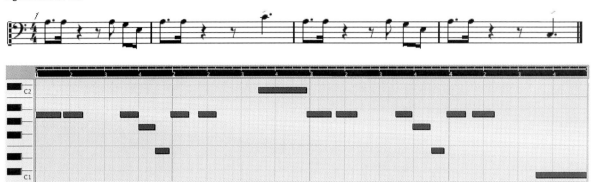

Figure 10.9 Bass line, Key Editor.

More could be done. Experiment with it yourself if you like. Congas, whistles … anything you fancy really!

Info

In the Drum Editor, below the drum sound list there is a drop-down menu where a GM drum map can be selected. The Drum Map Setup box can also be accessed from here.

Project 9: *Get Creative With Cubase* jingle

Musical objectives

- To construct a jingle in Dance Music style.
- Improvise a vocal line using the phrase 'Get Creative with Cubase.'

Cubase SX/SL skills

- Import and use a Rex File.
- Utilise the A1 Synth on three tracks.
- Apply EQ.
- Insert plug-ins: Double Delay and Compress.

Preparation

1　From the CD, copy the folder named 'project 9' to your desktop.
2　Inside the 'project 9' folder you'll find a file named 'template9.cpr'. Open it and use it for this project.
3　Create a folder in which to save your own files as you work through the project.

The assignment

Using a combination of audio loops and sequenced VST Instruments compose a short jingle suitable for use with the Get Creative Web Site. Record a vocal track chanting or singing the words 'Get Creative With Cubase'.

If you want to listen through the finished project file and find out how it goes load 9mix.cpr. If you have read chapter 3 – all about getting ideas and developing them – then you will understand the importance of knowing where you are heading. This is often best worked out away from the computer either in your head or sometimes as notes or sketches on paper.

Although the drum loop comes first in this project, it must be said that the idea for the vocal part came first. It was buzzing around in my head for weeks before I actually got around to recording it. Although it's the essence of the piece and everything else is built around it, for now, it can wait.

Info

The template has a time signature of 4/4 and the tempo is 120 bpm. Now this may be a bit fast for you. If so scroll the tempo to suit you. Mute the audio tracks when recording at a lower speed (they cannot be slowed with the MIDI tracks, apart from the drum track which uses a Rex file). When listening back, change the tempo to 120 bpm again.

175

Take 1

Track 1: Drums – mono audio track.
Toolbar: Snap to Bar.
Transport panel: (L) 1.01.01.

You are going to import a Rex File – donated by those fine purveyors of loops, Pocketfuel (www.pocketfuel.com).

Follow these steps:

1　Ensure that the project cursor is at 1.01.01, and from the project9/Audio folder import 89bpm.rex [File > Import > Audio File...]. Cubase creates an Audio Part containing several Audio Events in the Project window. The Rex file was originally recorded at 89bpm. The piece is set to 120 bpm. However, the file will play back at any tempo. Try it! Turn off the Master tempo first.

2　Repeat the part 24 times, as far as bar 25.

3　Save Project – compare with 9.1.cpr.

Info

When imported into Cubase SX/SL, Rex files (.rex) will play back at whatever tempo you decide to use. How does this work? Well, when 89bpm.rex is viewed in the Audio Part Editor (double click on part) you will notice that there are several audio slices (Figure P9.1). Slow the tempo to around 30 bpm and see how the slices become separated thus allowing the audio to play back at various speeds – even at this ludicrously slow tempo (Figure P9.2).

Figures P9.1 and P9.2 89bpm.rex and the same thing slowed down.

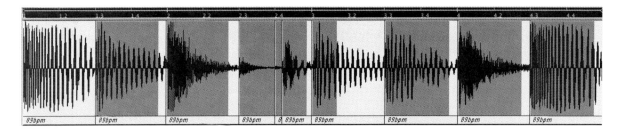

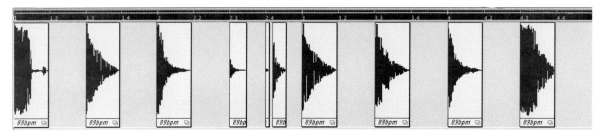

Take 2

Track 2: Bass.
Quantize Selector: 1/16 Note.
Inspector: [out: A1] [ch: 2] [program: Quintett JH].
Track Parameters: Transpose -12.
Transport panel: (L) 1.01.01 (R) 5.01.01.

Although the A1 synth has some very nice bass pre-sets I've chosen one of the others, Quintett JH. I wanted something in fifths here, to underpin the drum loop. You may prefer another, or you may want to experiment and edit the chosen pre-set. I did make one change to the pre-set by turning off the Chorus/Flanger section. A simple repetitive riff is all that's required.

Follow these steps:

1 Record the bass part between the locators (Figure P9.3 and P9.4).
2 Try adding a swing percentage in the Quantize Setup. I used 33%.
3 Repeat the part 5 times as far as bar 25.
4 Save Project – compare with 9.2.cpr.

Figure P9.3 Bass part.

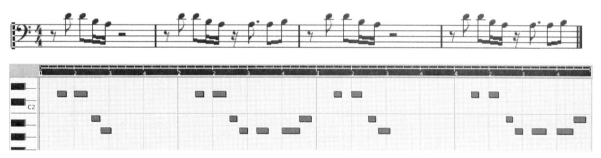

Figure P9.4 Bass part, Key Editor view..

Start thinking about where in the piece to put the 'Get Creative With Cubase' vocal line. Try improvising, either singing or chanting, along with the track. Even in this short space of nine bars there are endless possibilities. I know how my mine goes, it's been driving me nuts for days! However, before my forthcoming virtuoso vocal performance – another short loop. This time its funky guitar.

Take 3

Track 3: Guitar – stereo audio track.

Follow these steps:

1 Set the project cursor to 5.01.01, and from the project9/Audio folder import guitar.aif.
2 Repeat the new audio event (bars 5-6) between bars 7-8.
3 Save Project – compare with 9.3.cpr.

OK, there's a nice funky background as a basis for the vocal, bars 1 – 5 serving as an introduction. Now for the vocal. As I'm not too hot at singing, I decided to record my version in two takes, the first being 'Get Creative' and the second 'with Cubase.' This served my purposes fine, because I wanted the phrase split up between each guitar event.

At this point in the project you have the choice of recording your own improvised vocal or loading the audio files provided. It may be better to continue with mine (if you can stand it) and overdub yours later.

Take 4

Track 4: Vocal – mono audio track.

Follow these steps:

1 Set the project cursor at 5.01.01, and from the project9/Audio folder import getcreative.aif. Play it through. . . well, if you can do better, record your own!
2 Place the project cursor at 7.01.01, and from the project9/Audio folder import withcubase.aif.
3 The vocal can stand another repeat before boredom sets in so select the vocal events between bars 5 – 9 and repeat them once.
4 Save Project – compare with 9.4a.cpr.

The vocal between bars 5 – 13 has definitely run out of steam. However, before introducing something new it may be effective to repeat just the second phrase along with the guitar so:

1 Select the guitar and vocal events between bars 11 – 13 and repeat them once only, from 13 – 15.
2 Save Project – compare with 9.4b.cpr.

It's time for something new. Repetition and variation, remember. The drums and bass can chug on but another element or two are needed. Why not start with a moody synth line? – something simple that first climbs and then descends.

Take 5

Track 5: Synth.
Quantize Selector: 1/8 Note.
Inspector: [out: A1 2] [ch: 3] [program: Ensemble WMF].
Transport panel: (L) 15.01.01 (R) 23.01.01.

Follow these steps:

1 Record the synth part between the locators (Figures P9.5 and P9.6).
2 Select the recorded data in the Key Editor Edit window and apply Legato [MIDI > Functions > Legato]. Things have now taken a new direction with the synth creating a degree of tension.
3 Save Project – compare with 9.5.cpr.

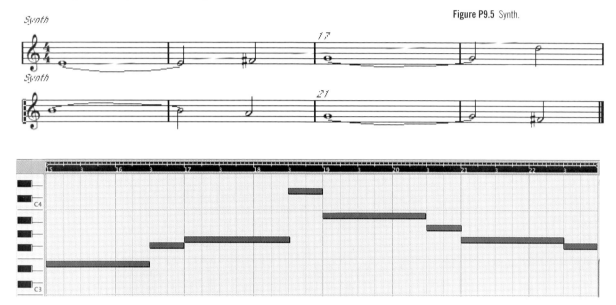

Figure P9.5 Synth.

Figure P9.6 Synth, Key Editor view.

I'm rather fond of simple two note pads for adding a touch of mystery. Placing it above the moving synth line will further establish the change of mood at measure 15.

Take 6

Track 6: Synth 2.
Quantize Selector: 1/8 Note.
Inspector: [out: A1 3] [ch: 4] [program: Coming In JH].
Track Parameters: Transpose 12.
Transport panel: (L) 15.01.01 (R) 23.01.01.

Follow these steps:

1 Record the synth 2 (Figures P9.7 and P9.8).
2 Save Project – compare with 9.6.cpr.

Figures P9.7 Synth 2.

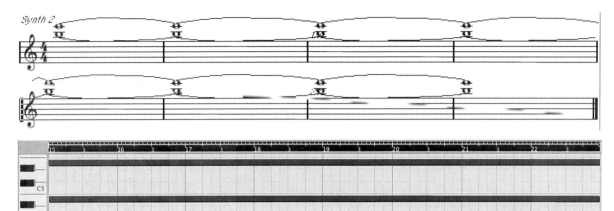

Figures P9.8 Synth 2, Key Editor view.

There's room for something else over those synth parts. Ask yourself what you can add. Sit back and listen. What comes to mind? You may well play guitar or some other instrument. If so it's time to 'Get Creative' and add something of your own. It is important though to try and hear what the piece needs first, before doodling commences. It need only be something very simple. What did I think of? Well I play saxophone and a very short jazz bebop motif kept nagging away in my head. It refused to budge and so I recorded it.

As with the vocal part, at this point in the project you have the choice of recording your own instrument. You may prefer to continue with my soprano sax and overdub something of your own later.

Take 7

Track 7: Soprano Sax – mono audio track.

Follow these steps:

1 Change Snap to Beat. Set the project cursor at 15.03.01, and from the project9 folder import the audio file soprano.aif.
2 Repeat the soprano event (bars 15.03.01-17.03.01) three times as far as bar 23.03.01.
3 Set the locators to (L) 1.01.01 (R) 23.01.01 and activate the Loop button. That's long enough for our purposes. Each cycle lasts 44 seconds.
4 Save Project – compare with 9.7.cpr.

The Mix

Load 9mix.cpr to hear and see a mix of 'Get Creative With Cubase'. Open the Mixer and look at the channels from left to right (Figure P9.9).

Figure 9.9 9mix.cpr, Mixer view.

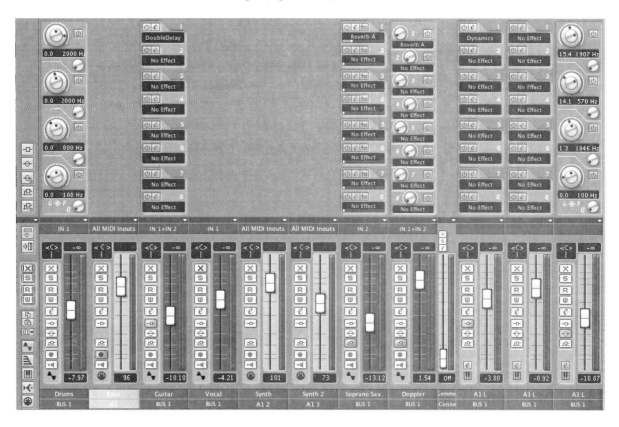

- Drums: this drum loop was already heavily processed at source, noticeably with phasing. Only volume is adjusted here.
- Bass: only volume is adjusted on this MIDI track because the audio signal is routed to the first of the A1 tracks. Any audio treatment with sends and inserts can be done from there.
- Guitar: a plug-in, Double Delay, has been inserted here. It works well because there's plenty of room for the delay to sound between the rather sparse guitar events themselves (Figure P9.10).

Figure P9.10 VST plug-in, Double Delay.

- Vocals: muted.
- Synth: only volume is adjusted on this MIDI track because the audio signal is routed to the second of the A1 tracks. Any audio treatment with sends and inserts can be done from there.
- Synth 2: only volume is adjusted on this MIDI track because the audio signal is routed to the third of the A1 tracks. Any audio treatment with sends and inserts can be done from there.
- Soprano Sax: Send effect Reverb A is used here.
- Doppler : 'What on earth's this,' you're probably thinking. You will remember that this piece evolved from the phrase 'Get Creative with Cubase' and that it had been rattling around in my head for some time before it was recorded. Well this is how I actually heard it. I could never sing it this way – or any other way, come to that – so I treated the track afterwards with the help of Steinberg's 'Doppler,' a VST plug-in included with their GRM Tools Vol. 2 (Figure P9.11). Doppler simulates the effect of a sound moving towards or away from you, and this also gives rise to an apparent change of pitch. Many strange effects are possible with a little experimentation.
- Compression was used carefully on the vocal before treatment with Doppler . Settings used – Ratio: 2:1 Threshold: -31dB Attack: 10.5ms
- Send effect Reverb A is used here too.

Figure P9.11 VST plug-in, Doppler.

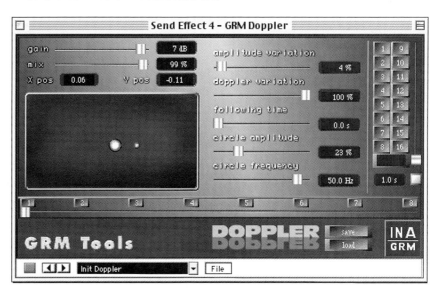

- A1 – Bass: The Dynamic plug-in has been inserted here and compression applied. Use the Bypass Insert button to audition the bass without it (Figure P9.12).
- A1 – Synth: Nothing extra here.
- A1 – Synth 2: No effects here, just some EQ. to bring out the high frequencies (Figure P9.13).

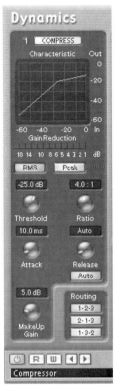

Figure P9.12 Compression.

Figure P9.13 EQ.

Why not experiment with EQ on this and other tracks? You can use the extended channel strip, (SX only) or use the Channel Settings window. Start the music and:

1 Click the Edit button on a Channel Strip (Figure P9.14) – the Channel Settings window opens (Figure P9.15).

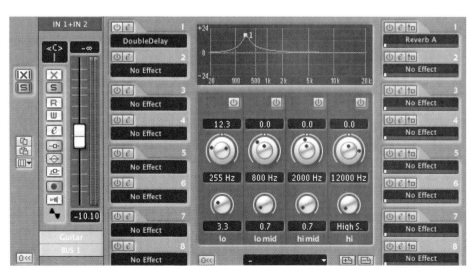

Figure P9.14 Edit button.

Figure P9.15 Channel Settings window.

2 Click in the EQ. curve display, above one of the four EQ. modules. A point appears corresponding to the module. Drag the point around, all the time listening to the change of tone. What you are doing here is altering the parameters for the activated EQ. module in question. Up to four of these points can be created. The EQ. parameters are:

- Gain (Figure P9.16) – affects the amount of boost or cut around a set frequency
- Frequency (Figure P9.17) – the centre frequency for the equalisation. Around this frequency, the sound will be boosted or cut depending on the gain.
- Q (Figure P9.18) – determines the width of the frequency band around the centre frequency. The narrower the frequency band, the more drastic the effect of the boost or cut.

Figure 9.16 EQ. gain control.
Figure 9.17 EQ. frequency control.
Figure 9.18 Q, frequency band control

Knowing the score

Rebecca's got the job. She's been sending demos and making follow up calls to a small independent TV production company in her area for some time now and they have finally given her a chance. They sent her a video. She composed some music using Cubase, mastered it to a CD and dropped it off personally. 'Great,' they said. 'How about a live version, played by real musicians?' 'No problem', replied Rebecca, 'I can print the score and parts direct from Cubase.' 'We'll book the studio and hire the session musicians,' they said. Rebecca went home a very happy person indeed.

A week later Rebecca arrives at the studio and peers through the control room window at the motley bunch of musicians sitting around drinking cups of coffee and reading newspapers. Scraps of conversation can be heard through the studio monitors. 'My central heating has bust again... I still haven't been paid for the last session we did here...'

Rebecca hands out the printed parts and listens nervously as the band begins a run through. 'It doesn't sound too good,' she thinks, 'I thought these guys could read and play anything that's put in front of them'. Pretty soon the band grinds to a halt.

'These parts are useless,' exclaims a particularly belligerent trumpet player. 'My part hasn't even been transposed.' 'We've all got different note lengths', bemoans the trombonist. 'My dog could write better parts than this!' growls the drummer.

So what did she do wrong? Although Rebecca can play piano, compose tunes and arrange them in Cubase, her music reading and writing skills lack professionalism. She made the all too common mistake of thinking that the notes she actually played into Cubase would appear correctly in the score printing and layout section of the program. What she had not realised is that in order for the music to be readable by musicians some editing is required. She played the original sequenced version to the musicians and after correcting the parts, they played it perfectly. Of course this took up valuable studio time and the session over ran by fifteen minutes. Overtime had to be paid to the musicians and studio owners.

It is important to understand the relationship between the Score Editor and the rest of the program. To begin with, it will not display the notes of recorded audio data. Not for the time being anyway. Maybe one day the technology will be able to handle it. No, the Cubase SX/SL Score Editor interprets recorded MIDI data and according to the settings you make, displays the result as conventional music notation.

Tip

To examine the Cubase Song files for this chapter, copy the folder named 'score' from the CD to your computer.

Tip

The Score Editor section of Cubase varies considerably between Cubase SL and Cubase SX. Basically, the SL version is much more limiting in its layout and printing facilities. For serious layout and printing use the SX version.

185

Before editing, every note recorded as MIDI data in Cubase is faithfully displayed in the Score Editor exactly as it was played. For example four bars of Jingle Bells – score/jingle.cpr – captured in Cubase displays like this (Figure 11.1). Looks wrong, doesn't it? But play it through and it sounds OK. The same data, after a little tweaking in the Staff Settings set-up box yields a perfect display (Figure 11.2). The MIDI data hasn't changed, just the interpretation.

Since this book is not a manual, At this point I would advise those readers who are unfamiliar with Cubase SX/SL Score Editor to study the documentation shipped with the program and work through the tutorials contained on the CD. Afterwards, proceed to the next chapter in this book, where a good many of the commonly used Score Editor features are used to format the music recorded in Project 6.

Figure 11.1

Figure 11.2

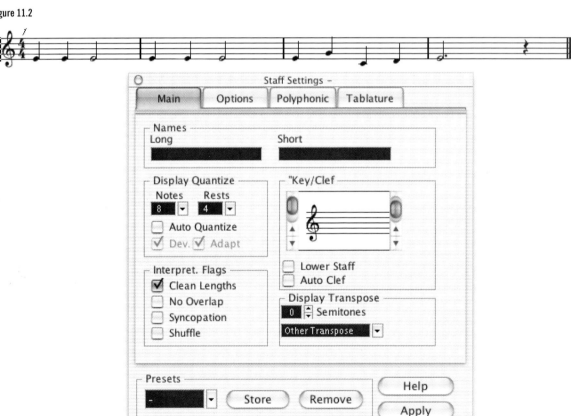

Project 10: Score cleanup

Musical objectives

- To transform an unintelligible mess into a readable score!

Cubase SX/SL skills

- Use the Staff Settings dialogue to: determine key signature and clef – choose Display Quantize and Interpretation Flag options for a clean score and correct notation – automatically display a transposed trumpet part.
- Use the Merge MIDI in Loop feature to create a single drum track from three separate tracks.
- Use Staff Pre-set feature to create a drum staff
- Use the Make Chords feature to automatically calculate and insert guitar chords.
- Use the Set Note Info dialogue to create 'slash style' chord symbols for the guitar part.
- Use the Symbol Palettes to insert slurs, accents, rehearsal marks, text and other markings.
- Use the Extended Toolbar to hide notes and rests and insert accidentals.
- Use the Layout Settings dialogue to – create a Score Layout – insert brackets to separate the brass and rhythm sections.
- Create a Pickup Bar.
- Insert title and copyright details.

Preparation

1 From the CD, copy the folder named 'project 10' to your desktop.
2 Inside the 'project 10' folder you'll find a file named 'template10.cpr.' Open it and use it for this project.
3 Create a folder in which to save your own files as you work through the project.

The assignment

The Football Theme, commissioned in Project 6, was a success. However, the program makers would like a studio version, played by real musicians. You need to prepare a score and printed parts for the session.

If you have already worked through Project 6 – A Football Theme – you will remember that it contained an audio track featuring yours truly on tenor sax. This has been deleted from the template. It was an improvised overdub and will not need scoring anyway. Besides, the company commissioning the music prefer the alternative solo trumpet (There's no accounting for taste!).

Follow these steps:

1 Rename the three brass tracks as Trumpets 1, 2, and 3 (Figure P10.1).
2 Select track 1/Trumpet 1 – including the events – and open the score. [MIDI > Open Score Editor] (Figure P10.2). From within the Score Editor select Page Mode [Scores > Page Mode]. From now on, when working on this score, use Page Mode.
3 You may be wondering why the track names are not displaying alongside the staves. To get them to show, open the Layout Settings dialogue [Scores > Layout Settings > Set-up...] and check the boxes named Show Staff Names and From Tracks. Press OK and all is revealed (Figure P10.3).
4 Save project – compare with 10.1.cpr.

Figure P10.1 Renaming brass tracks.

Figure P10.2 Trumpet 1 score.

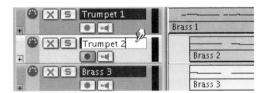

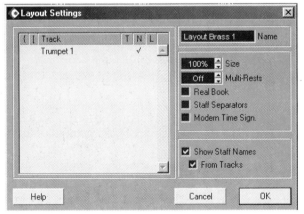

Figure P10.3 Layout Settings box.

Have a good look at the trumpet 1 score. What do you think? Your answers will vary according to how much knowledge of music notation you possess. If you can't read music at all it will not make much sense. In this case some time studying music theory is the only course of action open to you if you want to work with Cubase Score.

If you have experience of reading music at an entry or intermediate level, your answer might be: 'Looks all right to me. The first note is F followed by Bb and C. Yes I can understand that. Not sure about the rhythm though. It looks a bit funny.' In your case this project will help you display a decent, readable score.

If you are an experienced music reader your reaction will probably be something like: 'Well it is difficult to read because the key signature is missing and the note lengths are incorrectly displayed. There are no dynamic or articulation markings either.'

If you are a professional trumpet player your reaction may well be something like: 'Surely you don't expect me to read this rubbish!'

Follow these steps:

1 Keeping to the trumpet 1 track, from the Score Editor open the Staff Settings again [Scores > Staff Settings > Set-up...]. A dialogue box appears.
2 Click on the Polyphonic tab and in the Staff Mode section, ensure that 'Single' is selected.
3 The first things to change are the Display Quantize options. Our smallest note value in this piece is a 1/8th note so click on the Main tab and select that option in the Notes menu.
4 Select 4 from the Rests menu. Cubase will now only display rests smaller than this value where absolutely necessary. You can leave the Auto Quantize box unchecked in this case. The Interpretation Flags are also unnecessary here.
5 In the Key/Clef box, change the key to Bb (2 flats). The treble clef should be displayed already. If not, change it. The settings in the Staff Settings dialogue should now look like those in Figure P10.4.

Info

There are two ways of displaying the score: Edit Mode and Page Mode. Edit mode is ideal for musicians who read music fluently and prefer altering their MIDI data using conventional music notation. Page Mode is for preparing a score for printing and has many extra features.

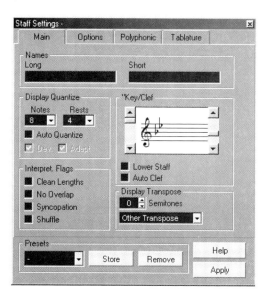

Figure P10.4 Staff settings.

Figure P10.5 Brass score layout.

6   Press Apply to see the changes. Yes, things are considerably improved. Gone are all the messy 16th notes and rests for starters (Figure P10.5).

7   Perform the same functions on the other two trumpet tracks.

8   Save Project – compare with 10.2.cpr.

That's the brass out of the way. For now anyway. Follow these steps:

1   Select the bass track (including the events) and open the score. Oh dear! This is enough to drive any self respecting bass player completely crackers! It's a jumble. Parts like this have been handed out though, believe me! (Figure P10.6).

Figure P10.6 Bass score.

2   From the Score, open the Staff Settings and as with the trumpet tracks, change the Display Quantize options to Notes: 8 and Rests: 4.

3   Alter the key to Bb and this time select the bass clef.

4   Press Apply to see the changes. What a difference! (Figure P10.7).

5   Save Project – compare with 10.3.cpr.

Conventional scores do not have separate drum staves. There are two here, kick and snare drum tracks plus a whistle on the referee track. Now combine them. Follow these steps:

1 Return to the Project window and mute all tracks except kick, snare and referee.
2 Set the locators to (L) 2.01. 01 (R) 37. 01. 01, to encompass the drum and referee tracks.
3 Create a new MIDI track and rename it Drums. Set the channel to 10 and map to GM.
4 With the new drum track selected, merge the un-muted tracks [MIDI > Merge MIDI in Loop] A new part entitled Merged should now appear on the drum track (Figure P10.8).

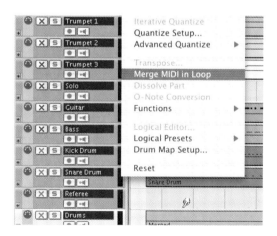

Figure P10.8 Drum track with Merged events.

5 With the new part selected, open the score and select the Drum Staff Pre-set [Scores > Staff Settings > jazz+pop > drumset]. If the General MIDI drum map has been selected in the Inspector, the drum clef will appear along with conventional drum notation: kick drum first space, and snare third space on the staff.
6 Open the Staff Settings dialogue and you will see that the Display Quantize options have been set to Notes: 16 and Rests: 4. Auto Quantize has been checked but can be turned off if you like as there are no triplets around. Leave

Clean Lengths checked (turn it off, press Apply and you will see why!). The drum score should appear as in Figure P10.9. Don't worry about the referee disappearing off the pitch! (bars 35 and 36) You'll get him back later.

Figure P10.9 Drum score.

7 Close the score, delete the old drums and referee tracks and un-mute the other tracks.

8 Save Project – compare with 10.4.cpr.

On to the guitar. Follow these steps:

1 Select the guitar track (including the events) and open the score (Figure P10.10). Well you can't give that to a guitar player. He'll fall about laughing! Apart from it being a jumble, what he requires here is a chord sheet. How do you do that? There are various methods. Here's one way to do it.

2 Open Staff Settings and change the Display Quantize options to Notes: 8 and Rests: 4.

3 Check the Clean Lengths box.

4 Change the key to Bb.

5 Check the Syncopation box. This cleans up all the notes that are tied across the beat. Click Apply to see the changes (Figure P10.11).

6 Save Project – compare to 10.5.cpr

Figure P10.10 Guitar score.

You are now going to add the chord symbols. Fortunately, you don't have to add a symbol above each chord manually, Cubase will do it for you.

Follow these steps:

Figure P10.11 A cleaner guitar score.

1 By clicking on the Make Chords Symbol icon on the extended tool bar (Figure P10.12) you can insert chord symbols above the changes. This also inserts the bass note of the chord. However in this case it's superfluous. So whilst performing Make Chords press Ctrl (Mac: Command) to insert chords without unnecessary bass notes.
2 The chords are inserted and left selected. Whilst still selected move them away from the notes to the beginning of each bar, for clarity. (Appropriate in this case because there is only one chord per bar).
3 Save Project – compare with 10.6.cpr (Figure P10.13).

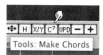

Figure P10.12 Make Chords Symbol icon.

Figure P10.13 Guitar score, with chord symbols.

Things are much clearer but the note display as well as chord symbols is superfluous. Follow these steps:

1 Delete all the notes except the bottom note on each stem.
2 Select all the notes [Edit > Select > All] and, whilst holding down the Ctrl (Mac: Command) key, change the pitch on the info line to F. All the notes now change to F. Note this cannot be achieved by dragging the notes in the score. Be sure to use the info line.
3 Select all the notes again and double click any note head. The Set Note Info dialogue box appears.
4 Change the Note Head option to a slash symbol (/) and click 'Apply.' All the note heads change to a slash symbol. (Figure P10.14).
5 Save Project – compare with 10.7.cpr.

Figure P10.14 Changing note heads.

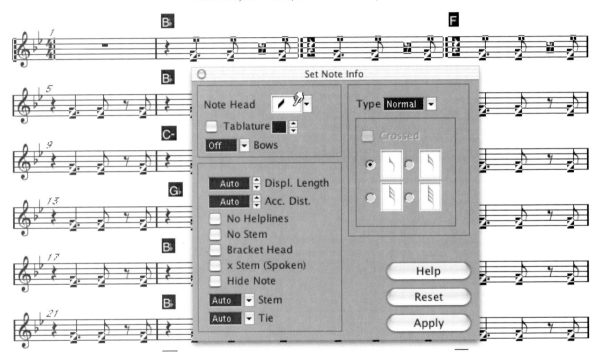

Figure P10.15 Inserting accents.

Musicians need more than just notes on the staff to correctly interpret a written piece of music. Articulation markings are particularly important.
    Follow these steps:

1 Return to the trumpet 1 track and open the score.
2 Click on the first note in bar 34 (Bb4). A glance at the Info line above will tell you that this note received more velocity than the note following. So did the note at 34. 02. 03. 010 (Ab4) They were clearly accented and you need to point this out to the trumpet player, so, select an accent (>) from the Note Symbol Palette [Scores >Symbol Palettes > Note Symbols] and apply it to those notes by clicking on their note heads (Figure P10.15).
3 Save Project – compare with 10.8.cpr

On viewing 10.8.cpr you will see that other accents and markings have been applied.

The slurs in bar 34 were added by first selecting the notes and using Scores > Staff Functions > Insert Slur (Figure P10.16).

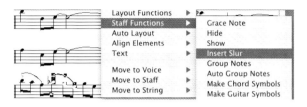

Figure P10.16 Inserting Slurs.

Although not strictly necessary, but courteous, the first note in bar 14 has been given a natural sign (cautionary accidental). This was applied by first selecting the note and clicking the '?' button on the Tool Bar (Figure P10.17).

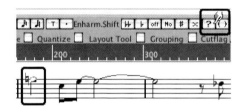

Figure P10.17 Adding an accidental sign.

OK, there's more to do. Follow these steps:

1 Change your version accordingly and Save Project.
2 Return to the bass track and open the score. The very last note is out of the bass player's range. (It was played here on a synth.) Move it an octave higher.
3 Return to the drum track and open the score. Time to get the referee back on the pitch by dragging him up to the top space of the stave. A cymbal note head appears, so now, indicate to the player that a whistle is required by entering text. [Scores > Symbol Palettes > Other > Text] (Figure P10.18).
4 Save Project – compare with 10.9.cpr.

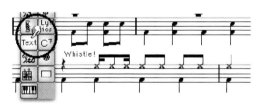

Figure P10.18 The whistle.

On to the score layout. Follow these steps:

1 In the Project window, select all the events on all tracks [Edit > Select > All].
2 Open the score. From the score, open the Layout Settings dialogue box [Scores > Layout Settings > Set-up...].
3 You are going to create a Layout for the full score. First check the Show Staff Names and From Tracks options.
4 Rename the Layout 'Full Score' and press OK to close the box (Figure P10.19).

Figure P10.19 Layout Settings, Full Score.

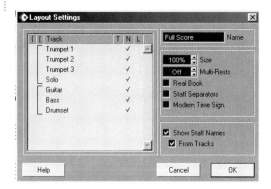

You can now call up the 'Full Score' layout at any time from the Score [Scores > Layout Settings > Show List... > Full Score].

5 Save Project – compare with 10.10.cpr.

On viewing 10.10.cpr you will see that other changes have taken place.

- Double bar lines have been inserted at the beginning of bars 2 and 18 – Double Click on bar line for menu – (Figure P10.20).
- The Brass and rhythm sections have been bracketed (Figure P10.21). This can be done with the Layout Symbols Palette. However these were added in the Layout Settings dialogue. There are columns for Braces and Brackets. Click in a column and drag downwards to select a group of tracks.
- The Solo Trumpet has been instructed to play an octave higher. [Scores > Symbol Palettes > Other > Text] (Figure P10.22).

Figure P10.20 (left) Altering bar lines.

Figure P10.21 (right) Adding staff brackets.

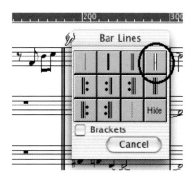

Figure P10.22 Adding text.

6 Change your version accordingly and Save Project.

Now prepare the trumpet 1 part. If you read the previous chapter 'Knowing the Score' you will remember the trumpet player complaining that his part had not been transposed. Our trumpet 1 part is in Bb at the moment. It will have to be transposed up a tone for performance purposes.

Follow these steps:

1 From within the Score Editor, select the Brass 1 Layout [Scores > Layout Settings > Layout Brass 1]. Open Staff Settings Set-up [Scores > Staff Settings > Set-up…].
2 In the Display Transpose section, select Trumpet from the menu. Press the Apply button and hey presto! the Trumpet 1 score has been transposed to the key of C (Figure P10.23).
3 Save Project – compare with 10.11.cpr.

Figure P10.23 Transposing instruments.

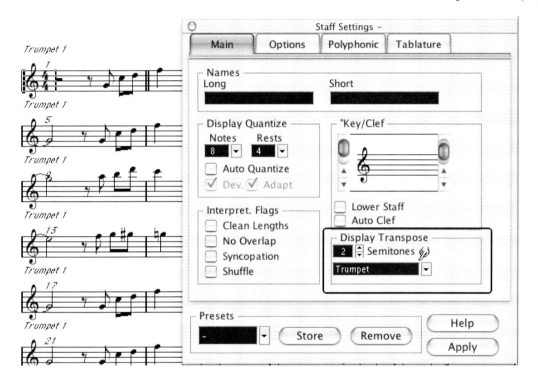

The first bar contains unnecessary rests. It's really a pickup bar. To modify it follow these steps:

1 Hide the rests with 'H' from the extended toolbar and drag the bar line to the left (Figure P10.24).
2 Reposition the notes using the Layout tool (Figure P10.25).
3 Click on the Bar 1 Number. A dialogue box opens. Enter an offset of -1. The pickup bar is now set to 0. This can be hidden with the 'H' symbol on the extended toolbar.
4 Save Project – compare with 10.12.cpr.

Info

Some writers prefer a transposed score, with all the instruments viewed in the keys that the actual players will read them. Others, myself included, prefer to view their scores in concert pitch.

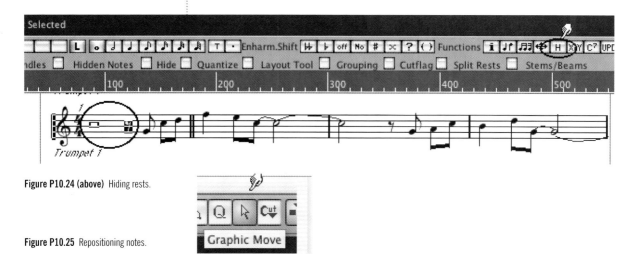

Figure P10.24 (above) Hiding rests.

Figure P10.25 Repositioning notes.

Figure P10.26 Global symbols (Page Text).

On viewing 10.12.cpr you will notice a number of other things:

- Title (top, centre page) and copyright details (top right) have been added using Global Page Text [Scores > Symbol Palettes > Global Symbols] (Figure P10.26). This type of text appears on all the layouts in a project. It's position on the page is fixed using the Layout Text dialogue box (Figure P10.27).
- Instrument names (top left) replace the track name details [Scores > Symbol Palettes > Layout]. This type of text is layout specific and will not appear on other pages. It's position on the page is fixed using the Layout Text dialogue box.

Figure P10.27 Layout Text dialogue box.

- Tempo has been indicated on all layouts using 'Tempo as note value' from the Layout Symbols (Figure P10.28).
- More accents and staccato markings have been applied to all the brass parts using Scores > Symbol Palettes > Note Symbols.
- All the brass parts are now transposed and display in the key of C.
- The drum part was littered with annoying rest symbols. They were cleaned up using the Hide symbol on the extended toolbar.

Much more can be done to improve this score, dynamic symbols for starters. Over to you!

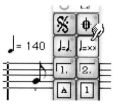

Figure P10.28 Indicating tempo.

Creative audio editing

Tim's frustrated. He's found the perfect drum loop for his latest project. Trouble is, for hours now he's been tearing his hair out trying to match the tempo of Cubase SX/SL with that of the loop. He's scrolled the tempo on Cubase SX/SL's transport panel with the mouse so many times that his arm is beginning to hurt. 'It's somewhere between 125 and 130 bpm', he mutters, 'but I'm dammed if I can nail it down'. Some time later (I'll not mention just exactly how long!) he finally settles on 127.2937bpm, but this is by no means certain. 'It'll have to do', he thinks.

Tim begins adding a bass line and a few keyboard licks to what seems a promising project. After a while he pauses to evaluate things and plays it through. 'Seems a bit slow', he thinks. 'It would be nice to move it up a notch or two'. He increases the tempo by several beats per minute. 'That's better. Wait a minute though, something sounds wrong. Of course, the audio doesn't fit now that I've altered the tempo. How am I going to fix it so that the audio follows my new tempo?', he asks himself. 'Oh well, back to the original tempo. What was it now? Oh no! I've forgotten. I think it was somewhere around 127 bpm'.

After much adjusting and readjusting, he finally settles on a tempo somewhere close to before but by now he's heard that drum loop dozens of times and he's rapidly going off it. 'That loop could do with a bit more swing', he mumbles. 'I wonder if I can quantize it, as I did with the MIDI tracks? I seem to remember reading something about this in the Cubase SX/SL manual. Oh well, I can't be bothered with all that'.

What has Tim done wrong? Well nothing really, apart from waste a lot of time fiddling about instead of fully reading the excellent documentation that's supplied with Cubase SX/SL. Had he done so he could have matched Cubase SX/SL's tempo to the drum loop in a fraction of the time it took him to do it manually, and far more accurately. He would also have discovered other useful and creative tools, such as the Time Stretch, Pitch Shift, Fade In, Fade Out, Reverse, Noise Gate and several more. As well as these processing functions there's also the option of using the VST plug-ins as well.

I tend to think of audio editing in two categories, functional and creative. Functional editing might include the business of cleaning up noisy tracks, altering audio levels, normalising and trimming. Creative audio editing may well include some of these features too, indeed functional and creative work constantly overlap. However creative audio editing is more likely to focus on altering the actual sound, pitch, length and even the 'feel' of audio files.

The following projects, 11 – 16, demonstrate just some of the wizardry possible when editing audio in Cubase SX/SL.

Project 11: Using hitpoints

Objective

- Match song tempo to audio by calculating the tempo of an imported audio file.
- Create ReCycle style audio loops that play back at any tempo

Cubase SX/SL skills

- Calculate hitpoints and slice a loop.
- Edit hitpoints.

Preparation

1 From the CD, copy the folder named 'project 11' to your desktop.

2 Inside the 'project 11' folder you'll find a file named 'template11.cpr.' Open it and use it for this project.

3 Create a folder in which to save your own files as you work through the project. This template contains a mono audio event (drumkit.aif) lasting just over four bars long. Take a glance in the Project window. 'That's odd. How is it that a four bar loop spans just over seven bars', I hear you mumble. Well, that's because you don't yet know the tempo of the loop itself. Our tempo on the Transport bar shows 120 bpm, but the loop's tempo is obviously slower. Before you record anything, MIDI or audio, it's best to determine the real tempo.

Follow these steps:

1 Select the audio event (drumkit) and from the Transport menu use 'Locators to Selection' to encompass it.

2 In the Sample Editor (double click on the event to open), define a four bar loop. Do this aurally at the audio file's tempo, not the Cubase SX/SL tempo. To do so, you will have to trim the audio event and eliminate the first rimshot, and the last snare beat. Adjust the event start and end points accordingly (Figure P11.1).

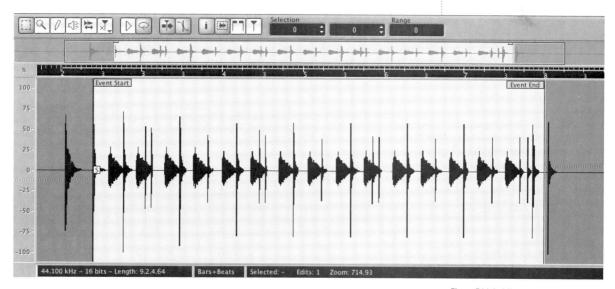

Figure P11.1 Adjusted start and end points.

3 Activate the Loop icon and press Play to audition the selection. If necessary make further adjustments to the loop until it's cycling smoothly.

4 You are now going to find the hitpoints in our loop and discover the tempo of the audio file. Click the Hitpoint Mode button on the Sample Editor toolbar (Figure P11.2). Hitpoints are calculated and now appear at the beginning of each sound in the loop (Figure P11.3). You'll also notice a Sensitivity slider and a series of drop down style menus on the toolbar (Figure P11.4). The 'Use' menu should be set to Sensitivity.

Figure P11.2 Hitpoint Mode button.

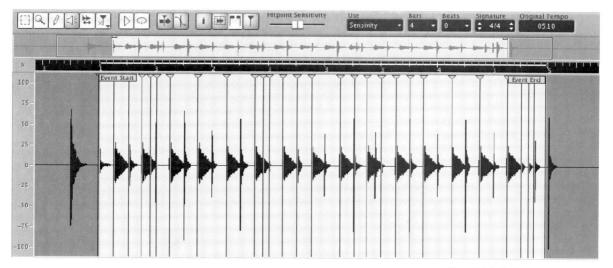

Figure P11.3 Hitpoints.

Figure P11.4 Hitpoint Sensitivity Slider and menus.

5 Enter the length of the loop (4 bars) in the Bars and Beats field and check that the time signature is set at 4/4 (Figure P11.5). The real tempo of the audio file is now displayed in the Original Tempo display. If you've done things correctly this will be 85 bpm or something very close. Mine came out at 85.10 bpm.

6 Save Project – compare to 11.1.cpr.

Figure P11.5 Bars and Beats field.

OK, you've established that the original tempo was 85 bpm. That's all well and good but our project tempo is still set to 120 bpm. Here's the clever bit. You are going to chop the file up into slices so that it can be played back at any speed you fancy.

Follow these steps:

1 Take a close look at your audio slices, between the hitpoints. If they are anything like mine – double hits in some of the slices – then editing is needed (Figure P11.6).

Figure P11.6 Double hits (shaded).

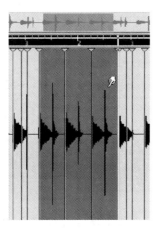

2 Audition the the individual slices between each hitpoint with the Speaker tool. The general idea is to have one sound to every slice. I could not achieve this with just the slider so I decided to edit them manually. To do this:

3 Zoom in on a slice with the Zoom tool and use the Pencil tool to divide the slice at the appropriate place (Figure P11.7). Audition the newly divided slices (Figure P11.8) afterwards, to check that they are how you want them.

4 OK, you're now ready to chop them up for real so slice the audio using 'Audio > Hitpoints > Create Audio Slices'.

5 The Sample Editor closes and the audio event is sliced at each hitpoint. This event is replaced, in the Project window, by an audio part containing the slices and the loop is automatically set to the Cubase SX/SL project tempo. In other words, if you press Play now it will play back perfectly at 120 bpm (even though it does sound slightly ridiculous!).

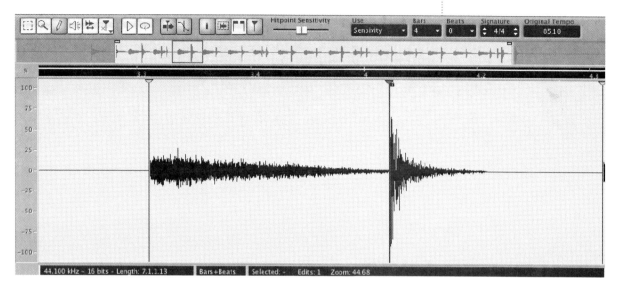

6 Move the audio part to bar 1 and set the locators between bars 1 and 5 and you can now play and loop the the audio back at just about any tempo you fancy, providing it's not too slow.

7 Save Project – compare with 11.1.cpr.

Figure P11.7 Dividing slices manually.

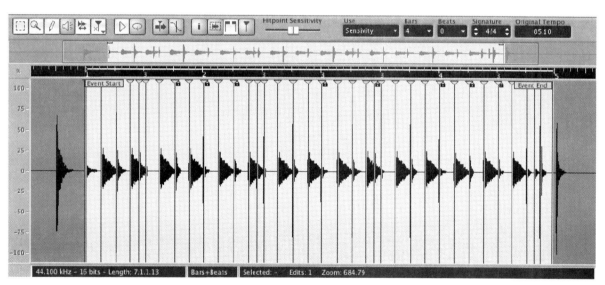

Figure P11.8 Slices after dividing.

Figure P11.9 Tracks containing sliced loops must be set to 'Musical time base' in the Track list or Inspector if you want to vary the tempo. The button shows a note symbol.

Figure P11.10 Gaps between slices at 60 bpm.

If the Cubase SX/SL tempo is lower than the loop's original tempo, there may well be audible gaps between the slices (Figure P11.10). Use 'Audio > Close Gaps' to remedy the situation (Figure P11.11).

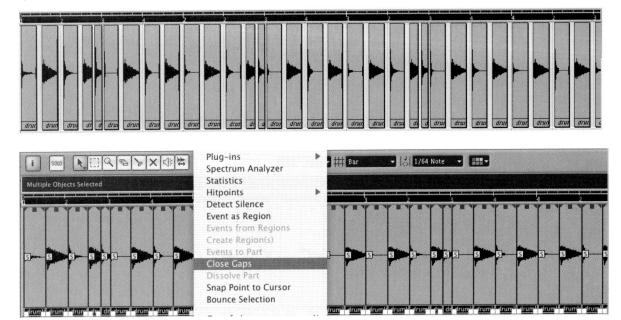

Figure P11.11 Gaps closed at 60 bpm.

There are seven ways to edit hitpoints:

- *Setting the sensitivity* using the Sensitivity slider to increase or reduce the number of hitpoints. As a rule, always try this method first.
- *Setting hitpoints according to note values* using the drop-down menu on the Sample Edit toolbar. Note values are selected and only hitpoints close to the selected value are used. The correct length of the loop must be set in the Bars and Beats field in the toolbar along with the time signature (Figure P11.12).
- *Disabling slices* using the Hitpoint Edit tool (Figure P11.13). In Disable mode the cursor changes to a cross. Clicking on the hitpoint's triangle disables the hitpoint itself. This is handy if you have too many hitpoints.
- *Locking slices* using the Hitpoint Edit tool in Lock mode. Use this when you have 'double hits' in one or several slices and increasing the sensitivity adds unwanted extra slices.
- *Setting hitpoints manually* using the Pencil tool to add missing slices (See above).

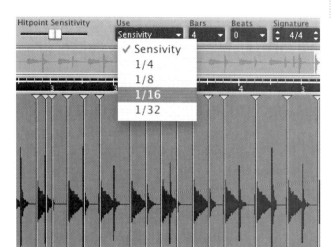

Figure P11.12 Hitpoints to note values.

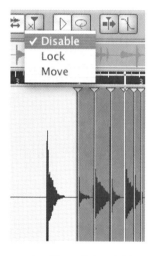

Figure P11.13 Disabling slices.

Tip

Don't delete hitpoints that were calculated by Cubase SX/SL. These are better left and disabled.

- *Moving hitpoints* using the Hitpoint Edit tool after manual editing. This might be needed if you have placed a hitpoint too far away from the start of a sound or in the sound itself.
- *Deleting hitpoints* using the Hitpoint Edit tool in Move mode to drag a hitpoint from the Sample Edit window.

There are more creative possibilities to explore by opening the Audio Part Editor. Double click on the new audio part to open it. From here you can experiment. Try the following:

- Muting slices with the Mute tool.
- Change the order of the slices to create a new drum pattern.
- Quantize the slices – see Project 12.
- Process the slices – see Project 13.

Project 12: Quantizing audio loops

Objective

- Hard quantize a sliced audio loop with a 16th note feel to that of an 8th note swing feel.

Cubase SX/SL skills

- Use the Quantize Setup box.
- Use the Close Gaps feature.

Preparation

1 From the CD, copy the folder named 'project 12' to your desktop.
2 Inside the 'project 12' folder you'll find a file named 'template12.cpr.' Open it and use it for this project.
3 Create a folder in which to save your own files as you work through the project. This template picks up where project 11 left off and contains a five bar drum loop that's been sliced using the hitpoints feature (Figure P12.1). You can do various creative things using these slices. In this project you'll use the Quantize Setup box to change the feel of the loop.

Figure 12.1 Sliced audio.

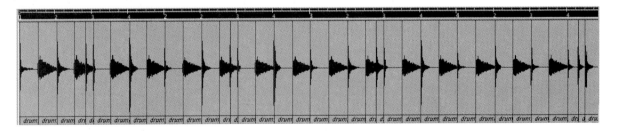

Follow these steps:

1 Select the loop and double click to open the Audio Part Editor. Open the Quantize Setup box [MIDI > Quantize Setup...] (Figure P12.2).
2 You are going to make a radical change to the feel of this loop so: Within the Quantize Setup, set the Grid Quantize to 1/8, the Type to Straight and apply 70% Swing. Press the Apply button. Quite a change takes place. Play it

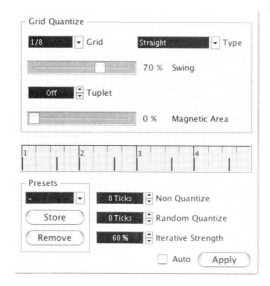

Figure P12.2 Quantize Setup.

through and you'll notice the off-beat 16th notes have disappeared and the hi-hat beats are later, due to the applied swing value (Figure P12.3).

3 You'll have noticed the gaps between many of the slices. These gaps are audible (not too bad, a kind of gated effect). To create a smoother effect: Select all the slices and apply Close Gaps [Audio > Close Gaps]. This function applies time stretching to the audio contained in each slice and does exactly what one expects it to – closes the gaps (Figure P12.4).

4 Save project – compare with 12.1.cpr.

Figure 12.3 Quantized slices.

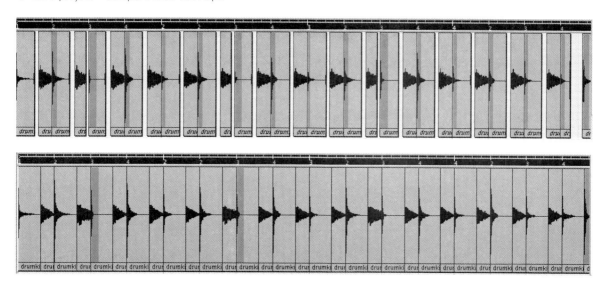

Figure 12.4 Gaps closed.

Incidentally, this project sounds good at a faster tempo. Just deactivate the Master button and scroll the tempo.

Project 13: Processing slices

Objective

- To enhance the individual slices of a drum loop with various plug-ins.

Cubase SX/SL skills

- Use the Audio Part Editor to process audio slices.
- Use plug-ins: Reverb A and Metalizer.
- Use processor, Gain.

Preparation

1 From the CD, copy the folder named 'project 13' to your desktop.
2 Inside the 'project 13' folder you'll find a file named 'template13.cpr'. Open it and use it for this project.
3 Create a folder in which to save your own files as you work through the project.

This template picks up where project 11 left off and contains a five bar drum loop that's been sliced using the hitpoints feature. You can do various creative things using these slices. In this project you'll add some effects to individual slices. Some reverb on the snare hits would be nice.

Follow these steps:

1 Select the loop and double click to open the Audio Part Editor. Use the Speaker tool to audition the slices and select all the snare hits.
2 With the snare hits selected, open Reverb A [Audio > Plug-ins > reverb > Reverb A] and choose a pre-set. Edit the pre-set if you like and audition the effect with the Preview button. When happy use the Process button. All the snare hits are now treated with reverb (Figure P13.1).
3 Now, those hi-hat slices are a little on the quiet side. Let's make them louder. Find all the hi-hat slices and, in the same way, process them with Gain [Audio > Process > Gain]. Raise the level by 5.00 dB. That should beef the hi-hat up a little (Figure P13.2).
4 Now go one step further and process the hi-hat with Metalizer or anything else that takes your fancy (Figure P13.3).
5 Save project – compare with 13.1.cpr.

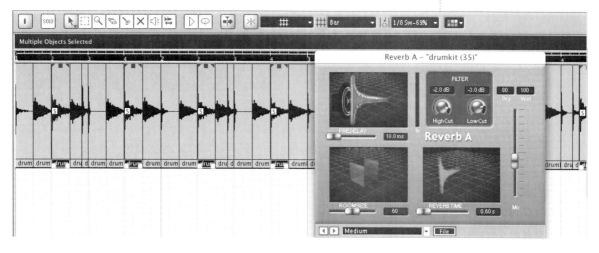

Figure P13.1 Snare hits with Reverb A.

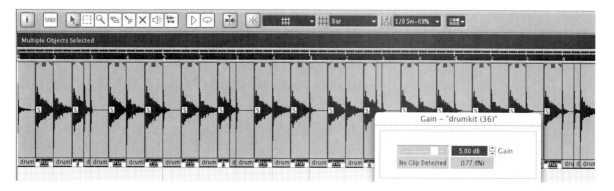

Figure P13.2 Hi-hats, with Gain raised.

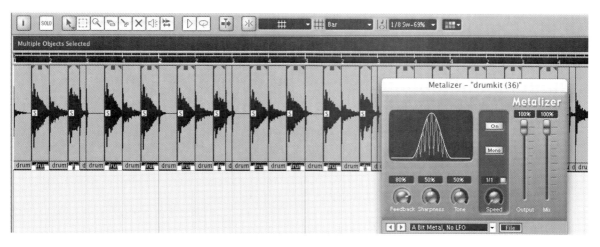

Figure P13.3 Hi-hats with Metalizer.

Project 14: Creating a Groove Quantize Map

Objective

- Extract a groove from an audio file and apply it to MIDI material.

Cubase SX/SL skills

- Use Hitpoints feature and Create Groove Quantize.

Preparation

1 From the CD, copy the folder named 'project 14' to your desktop.
2 Inside the 'project 14' folder you'll find a file named 'template14.cpr'. Open it and use it for this project.
3 Create a folder in which to save your own files as you work through the project.

This template contains a two bar drum loop and contains clear 16th note beats on the kick drum. The plan here is to create 16th note hitpoints, extract the groove and apply it to a MIDI drum loop (Figure P14.1).

Figure P14.1 template14.cpr.

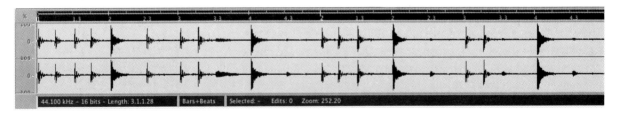

Follow these steps:

1 On track 2, sequence this simple drum pattern (Figures P14.2 and P14.3). Keep it straight and quantize to 1/16 Note. This is in effect a simplified version of the audio drum loop on track 1. The tricky hi-hats have been left out!
2 Play the audio and MIDI loop together and you'll hear that things are not exactly synchronised. To remedy that:
3 Select the audio event (16kicks) and from the Transport menu use 'Locators to Selection' to encompass it.
4 On track 1, double click on the audio event to open the Sample Edit window. Click the Hitpoint Mode button on the Sample Editor toolbar. Hitpoints are

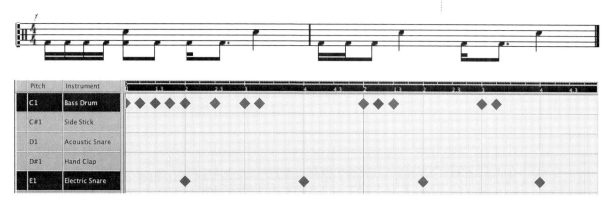

calculated and now appear at the beginning of each sound in the loop. The 'Use' menu should be set to 1/16 and the 'Bars" menu set to 2 (Figure P14.4).

Figure P14.2 (top) Drum pattern.
Figure P14.3 Drum pattern, Drum Editor view.

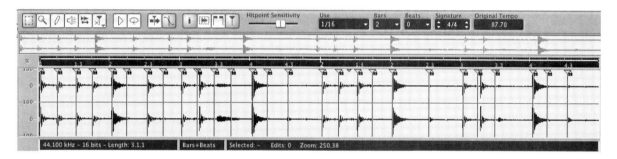

Figure P14.4 1/16 Hitpoints.

5 Now extract the groove [Audio > Hitpoints > Create Groove Quantize].
6 Pull down the Quantize pop-up in the Project window and you'll find an additional item at the bottom of the list, with the same name as the file from which you extracted the groove – 16kicks Sliced (Figure P14.5).
7 Apply this new groove – 16kicks Sliced – to the MIDI drum loop you created on track 2. Play the audio and MIDI tracks simultaneously and you'll find things are much more together. The audio groove has been imposed on the MIDI loop. There's room for improvement, but this can be improved with a little editing.
8 Save Project – compare with 14.1.cpr.

Tip

Although Cubase SX/SL does a pretty good job of extracting a groove from audio material, unlike the previous VST version, there's no way of extracting a groove from MIDI material – or is there? Simply re-record your MIDI loops as audio first. Problem solved!

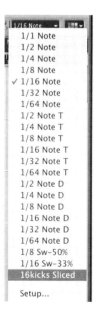

Figure P14.5 New groove – 16kicks Sliced.

Project 15: Audio pitch shifting

Objective

- Create a sax section from a single sax audio file.

Cubase SX/SL skills

- Use Pitch Shift.

Preparation

1 From the CD, copy the folder named 'project 15' to your desktop.
2 Inside the 'project 15' folder you'll find a file named 'template15.cpr'. Open it and use it for this project.
3 Create a folder in which to save your own files as you work through the project.

This template contains an audio event, a few bars of alto sax playing a jazz waltz. How about turning this into a sax section with harmonies? It can be done quite quickly with Pitch Shift (Figure P15.1).

Follow these steps:

1 Select the audio event on track 1 and drag a copy to track 2.
2 Open the Pitch Shift dialogue box [Audio > Process > Pitch Shift]. We are going to transpose this event up a fourth. That's five semitones. So, enter a value of 5 in the Pitch Shift Settings section. Use the Preview button to audition the pitch change. What do you think? Sounds remarkably like a soprano saxophone to me. Let's make a commitment. Press the Process button. and
3 Now play the two tracks together. Sounds fine to me. How about a tenor sax underneath the soprano and alto?
4 Drag another copy of the event from track 1 to track 3.
5 This time set a Transpose value of -7. That's a fifth lower. Audition with the Preview button. Opinions? Well it doesn't sound like a tenor sax. However, it does sound remarkably like a baritone sax. That's OK with me. Press the Process button.
6 Now play all three tracks together. Instant sax section!
7 Save Project – compare with 15.1.cpr.

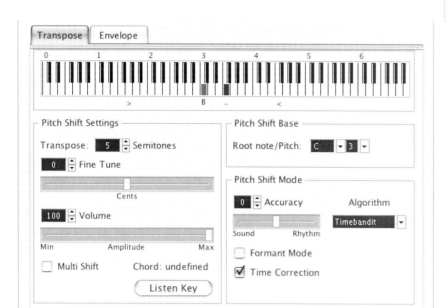

Project 16: Audio time stretching

Objective

- Time stretch an audio file to fit the existing tempo.
- Time stretch an audio file to fit a slower tempo.

Cubase SX/SL skills

- Use the Time Stretch tool in the Project window.
- Use the Time Stretch dialogue box.

Preparation

1 From the CD, copy the folder named 'project 16' to your desktop.
2 Inside the 'project 16' folder you'll find a file named 'template16.cpr'. Open it and use it for this project.
3 Create a folder in which to save your own files as you work through the project.

In the previous project Pitch Shift was used to alter the pitch of an audio file and create harmonies. In this project you will use the same file but this time first, stretch it to fit an existing tempo and secondly, stretch it to fit a slower tempo. Both times without altering the pitch.

Follow these steps:

Figure P16.1 'Sizing applies timestretch'.

1 Click on the Arrow on the Project window toolbar and choose 'Sizing applies timestretch' from the drop-down menu (Figure P16.1).
2 Select the audio event and stretch the part as far as bar 11 or 12 by dragging the right hand lower corner.
3 Release the mouse button and the audio is stretched to fit the new part length. That's it. So easy.
4 Save Project – compare with 16.1.cpr.

Time stretching an audio event to fit a predetermined tempo, without altering its pitch can be done using the Time Stretch dialogue box.

Re-load template16.cpr and follow these steps:

1 Select the audio event and open the Time Stretch dialogue [Audio > Process > Time Stretch] (Figure P16.2).
2 The Input section (left) displays the project tempo as 197 bpm. Change the Out put tempo (right) to 170 bpm. As you alter the output tempo you'll notice the Length in Samples and Length in Seconds displays will change accordingly. So too will the Time Stretch percentage display. Conversely, changing the percentage display will also be reflected in the other displays.
3 Press the Process button and return to the Project window. The audio event has been stretched.
4 On the transport panel, deactivate the Master tempo and scroll the tempo to 170 bpm. You're done. Quite simple really.
5 Save project – compare with 16.2.cpr.

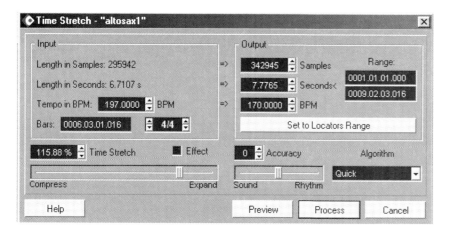

Tip

Imported audio files do not always fit exactly to bar lengths and using the Repeat function to create loops will sometimes leave small, audible gaps between the parts. Time stretching them first, with the arrow tool, will make them easier to repeat seamlessly.

Figure P16.2 Time Stretch dialogue.

Appendix 1
Instrument ranges

Use these as a guide when emulating real instruments with MIDI. These are safe, practical ranges, used when writing for real players. For a realistic interpretation avoid the high and low extremes except perhaps for solo passages.

Guitar E1 – E4

Bass Guitar E0 – G2

Trumpet E2 – Bb4

Trombone E1 – Bb3

Bass Trombone C1 – F3

Alto Saxophone Db2 – Ab4

Tenor Saxophone Ab1 – Eb4

Baritone Sax Db1 – Ab3

Soprano Sax Ab2 – Eb5

Flute C3 – C6

Piccolo D4 – Bb6

Oboe Bb2 – F5

Clarinet D2 – G5

Bassoon Bb0 – Bb3

French Horn B0 – F4

Appendix 2
Key commands

File commands

	Windows	*Mac*
New	Ctrl+N	Command+N
Open	Ctrl+O	Command+O
Close	Ctrl+W	Command+W
Save	Ctrl+S	Command+S
Save New Version	Ctrl+Alt+S	Command+Option+S
Save As	Ctrl+Shift+S	Command+Shift+S
Quit	Ctrl+Q	Command+Q

Devices

	Windows	*Mac*
Mixer	F3	F3
VST Outputs	F4	F4
VST Inputs	F5	F5
VST Send Effects	F6	F6
VST Master Effects	F7	F7
Video	F8	F8

Transport commands

	Windows	*Mac*
Show/hide Transport panel	F2	F2
Start	Enter	Enter
Stop	Pad 0	Pad 0
Start/Stop	Space	Space
Record	Pad *	Pad *
Rewind	Pad -	Pad -
Fastwind	Pad +	Pad +
Return to Zero	Pad .	Pad .
Cycle on/off	Pad /	Pad /
Auto Punch In on/off	I	I
Auto Punch Out on/off	O	O
Play Selection Range	Alt+Space	Option+Space
Locate Next Event	N	N
Locate Previous Event	B	B

Locators to Selection	P	P
Locate Selection	L	L
Loop Selection	Shift+G	Shift+G
Nudge Up	Ctrl+Pad +	Command+Pad +
Nudge Down	Ctrl+Pad -	Command+Pad -
To Left Locator	Pad 1	Pad 1
To Left Locator	Shift+1	Shift+1
To Right Locator	Pad 2	Pad 2
To Right Locator	Shift+2	Shift+2
To Markers 3 to 9	Pad 3 to 9	Pad 3 to 9
To Markers 3 to 9	Shift+3 to 9	Shift+3 to 9
Locate Next Marker	Shift+N	Shift+N
Locate Previous Marker	Shift+B	Shift+B
Set Left Locator	Ctrl+Pad 1	Command+Pad 1
Set Left Locator	Ctrl+ 1	Command+ 1
Set Right Locator	Ctrl+Pad 2	Command+Pad 2
Set Right Locator	Ctrl]+ 2	Command+ 2
Set Marker 3 to 9	Ctrl+Pad 3 to 9	Command+Pad 3 to 9
Set Marker 3 to 9	Ctrl+ 3 to 9	Command+ 3 to 9
Input Position	Shift+P	Shift+P
Input Left Locator	Shift+L	Shift+L
Input Right Locator	Shift+R	Shift+R
Insert Marker	Insert	Insert
Metronome (Click) on/off	C	C
Sync Online on/off	T	T

Editing and editor commands

	Windows	Mac
Undo	Ctrl+Shift+Z	Command+Shift+Z
Redo	Ctrl+Shift+Z	Command+Shift+Z
Cut	Ctrl+X	Command+X
Copy	Ctrl+C	CtrlCommand+C
Paste	Ctrl+V	Command+V
Delete	Del, Backspace	Del, Backspace
Select All	Ctrl+A	Command+A
Select None	Ctrl+Shift+A	Command+Shift+A
Autoscroll on/off	F	F
Snap on/off	J	J
Duplicate	Ctrl+D	Command+D
Open	Ctrl+E	Command+E
Repeat	Ctrl+K	Command+K
Lock	Ctrl+Shift+L	Command+Shift+L
Unlock	Ctrl+Shift+U	Command+Shift+U
Cut Time	Ctrl+Shift+X	Command+Shift+X
Delete Time	Shift+Back	Shift+Back
Paste Time	Ctrl+Shift+V	Command+Shift+V
Paste at Origin	Alt+V	Option+V
Split Range	Shift+X	Shift+X
Insert Silence	Ctrl+Shift+E	Command+Shift+E
Split at Cursor	Alt+X	Option+X
Move to Cursor	Ctrl+L	Command+L

Solo	S	S
Mute	M	M
Record Enable	R	R
Quantize	Q	Q
Mute Events	Shift+M	Shift+M
Unmute Events	Shift+U	Shift+U
Mute/Unmute Objects	Alt+M	Option+M
Open Score Editor	Ctrl+R	Command+R
Open/Close Editor	Return	Return
Left selection side to Cursor	E	E
Right selection side to Cursor	D	D
Show/Hide Inspector	Alt+1	Option+1
Show/Hide Infoview	Ctrl+1	Command+1
Show/Hide Overview	Alt+0	Option+0

Audio editing commands

	Windows	Mac
Crossfade	X	X
Find selected in Pool	Ctrl+F	Command+F
Adjust Fades to Range	A	A

Nudge, select and navigate

	Windows	Mac
Nudge Start Left	Ctrl+Left	Command+Left
Nudge Start Right	Ctrl+Right	Command+Right
Nudge End Left	Alt+Left	Option+Left
Nudge End Right	Alt+Right	Option+Right
Navigate/Select Left	Left	Left
Navigate/Select Right	Right	Right
Navigate/Select Up	Up	Up
Navigate/Select Down	Down	Down
Add Left	Shift+Left	Shift+Left
Add Right	Shift+Right	Shift+Right
Add Up	Shift+Up	Shift+Up
Add Down	Shift+Down	Shift+Down

Zoom commands

	Windows	Mac
Zoom In	H	H
Zoom Out	G	G
Zoom to Selection	Alt+S	Option+S
Zoom to Event	Shift+E	Shift+E
Zoom Full	Shift+F	Shift+F
Zoom In Tracks	Alt+Down	Option+Down
Zoom Out Tracks	Alt+Up	Option+Up
Zoom Out Tracks	Ctlr+Up	Command+Up
Zoom Tracks Exclusive	Z	Z
Zoom Tracks Exclusive	Ctrl+Down	Command+Down

Tool commands

	Windows	Mac
Previous Tool	F9	F9
Next Tool	F10	F10
Select Tool	1	1
Range Tool	2	2
Split Tool	3	3
Glue Tool	4	4
Delete Tool	5	5
Zoom Tool	6	6
Mute Tool	7	7
Draw Tool	8	8
Play Tool	9	9
Drumstick Tool	0	0

Project menu commands

	Windows	Mac
Open Pool	Ctrl+P	Command+P
Open Markers	Ctrl+M	Command+M
Open Master Track	Ctrl+T	Command+T
Open Browser	Ctrl+B	Command+B
Project Setup	Shift+S	Shift+S

Window Layout commands

	Windows	Mac
New	Ctrl+Pad 0	Command+Pad 0
Recapture	Alt+Pad 0	Option+Pad 0
Organize	W	W
Layout 1 to 9	Alt+Pad 1 to 9	Option+Pad 1 to 9

Index

Fast Guide to Cubase SX

Simon Millward

420 pp • 244 x 172 mm
ISBN 1870775 83 X • £22.95

* Installation and setting up
* Audio and MIDI recording and editing
* Mixing, EQ and effects
* Hands on projects
* Time saving shortcuts
* For Cubase SX and SL

Cubase SX is a radical new Cubase which takes professional software-based music creation and production into the 21st century. The digital desktop recording studio is now, more than ever, a reality and Steinberg have managed to streamline the operation of SX so that it is faster and more logical to use while also increasing its power and flexibility.

The Fast Guide to Cubase SX provides all the information you need to quickly master the essentials of the software and also explores advanced techniques. The book covers all the important aspects of the program including recording and editing in the Project window, mixing in the Mixer, audio looping and editing in the Sample editor, and detailed MIDI editing in the the MIDI editors. Installation and setting up are explained and detailed information on audio and MIDI recording techniques, EQ, compression, gating, limiting, effects and mix automation are all featured. Projects throughout the book describe Cubase SX in a number of recording and editing situations, providing valuable practical insights into how best to use the program for specific tasks.

The Fast Guide to Cubase SX is not a retread of the manual. It is designed to be the ideal companion to Steinberg's user documentation and suits all levels of users, from the home sound recordist/musician to the advanced audio professional.

Simon Millward is a music software specialist and sound designer. He has a Master of Science degree in Music Technology from the University of York, UK. Originally trained as a musician and subsequently as a sound engineer, his interest in software sequencers and virtual studio instruments has established him as one of the UK's foremost Cubase experts

PC Publishing

Export House, 130 Vale Road, Tonbridge, Kent TN9 1SP, UK
Tel 01732 770893 • Fax 01732 770268 • e-mail info@pc-publishing.com
Website http://www.pc-publishing.com

Check our website!
www.pc-publishing.com

Sound Synthesis with VST Instruments

Simon Millward

277 pp • 244 x 172 mm • illustrated
ISBN 1870775 73 2 • £19.95

- For PC or Apple Mac
- Build your own software synth
- Synthesize new sounds with VST Instruments
- Create a virtual electric guitar
- Tips on using VST Instruments
- Compatible with all host software applications

VST instruments offer an unprecedented opportunity for the exploration of sound and musical creativity. The world of hi-tech music and audio has never been so full of possibilities for experimentation and the creation of new sounds. Sound synthesis instruments which were once prohibitively expensive are now available to everyone in the form of cost-effective software.

Sound Synthesis with VST Instruments helps you realise your own musical creativity by exploring the theory of sound synthesis and linking this to practical examples in the virtual world of VST instruments. It explains how creating your own original synth patches can inspire a whole new musical composition, how building your own software synthesizer can be the beginning of a new adventure into the world of sound synthesis, and how manipulating and processing samples in revolutionary ways can be the birth of the next cutting-edge dance track.

With practical projects, helpful tips, step-by-step instructions on how to build your own software synthesizer and virtual electric guitar, and in-depth coverage of Reaktor, Tassman, HALion, FM7, B4, Pro-52, LM4-MkII, Attack and many others, Sound Synthesis with VST instruments will be of particular interest to musicians, sound synthesists, sound designers, music producers and audio professionals.

PC Publishing
Export House, 130 Vale Road, Tonbridge, Kent TN9 ISP, UK
Tel 01732 770893 • Fax 01732 770268 • e-mail info@pc-publishing.com
Website http://www.pc-publishing.com

Check our website!
www.pc-publishing.com

Emagic Logic Virtual Instruments

Stephen Bennett

224 pp • 236 x 189 mm • illustrated
ISBN 1870775 84 8 • £14.95

- Set up and use Logic Virtual Instruments
- Learn how to get the sounds you want
- Use Virtual Instruments in your own songs
- Packed with 'how-to' features
- Step by step projects
- Tips and tricks

Emagic Logic is shipped with several virtual instruments. Though similar to VST instruments (VSTi), they are available only for Logic and thus have been written to tightly integrate with the sequencer and preserve precious CPU resources. Some of these are free with the program and some need to be purchased from Emagic. They range from simple to complex synthesisers alongside virtual emulations of several classic keyboards.

This book covers the set-up and use of these Logic Instruments, along with tips and tricks. There are many 'how to do' features and the book comes complete with hundreds of illustrations and step-by-step diagrams.

There are sections on Instrument purchase, demos and installation, using the Instruments within Logic, making the most of CPU power and using the Instruments during a mix down.

The book has many programming guides and advice on how to get certain sounds and use them in your own songs. It's the ideal companion book to Making Music with Logic Audio and will help you get the most from Logic Virtual Instruments.'

Stephen Bennett is a musician and writer based in Norwich, England. Apart from the series of Logic Audio books for PC Publishing, he has written for Sound on Sound *magazine and currently has a monthly Logic Audio feature in* Future Music.

PC Publishing

Export House, 130 Vale Road, Tonbridge, Kent TN9 1SP, UK
Tel 01732 770893 • Fax 01732 770268 • e-mail info@pc-publishing.com
Website http://www.pc-publishing.com

Check our website!
www.pc-publishing.com

Guitarist's Guide to Computer Music

Robin Vincent

239 pp • 236 x 189 mm • illustrated
ISBN 1870775 87 2 • £12.95

- Record guitar on your home PC
- Use your PC as an effects box
- Record a whole band or create a virtual one
- Creating drum patterns
- With CD of demo software and tutorials

'All this computer music nonsense is to do with electronic bleeps, silly noises and dance music isn't it?'

You couldn't be more wrong. A computer is far more suited to recording live 'real' music than anything else. Whether you play jazz, rock, punk, blues, folk, pop, classical, bluegrass or skiffle, the computer is the perfect tool for recording real instruments. There's nothing technical or mysterious about it, it can be exactly the same as recording to tape but with the added advantage of having an endless supply of effects, drums, backing and mixing, and at the end of the session you can put your music straight onto CD.

'But I like all my hardware gear'

Then you can keep it. A computer will add to your musical arsenal not take anything away, so you can use your existing gear together with the computer and this book will show you how.

Included with the book is a CD containing a fully working demo version of Steinberg's studio recording software Cubase SX, and other useful bits like software guitar effects and a tuner. This book will take you through the easy steps of recording and producing music on your computer, with example songs and detailed illustrations to remove any doubts or confusion over what can actually be achieved.

PC Publishing

Export House, 130 Vale Road, Tonbridge, Kent TN9 1SP, UK
Tel 01732 770893 • Fax 01732 770268 • e-mail info@pc-publishing.com
Website http://www.pc-publishing.com

Check our website!
www.pc-publishing.com

Get Creative with Emagic Logic

Keith Gemmell

218 pp • 244 x 172 mm • illustrated
ISBN 1870775 82 1 • £16.95

- For PC and Mac
- With CD of Logic and audio files
- Compose, arrange, record and mix your music
- Learn by doing with practical projects
- Record and edit with MIDI

Interested in composing – maybe for film and TV? Want to learn how to sequence, record and mix effectively with Emagic Logic? This project based book and CD will help you do both in a practical and enjoyable way. After all, much of today's commercial music is produced using little more than the composer's creativity harnessed with power of Emagic Logic production software.

The goals of Get Creative with Emagic Logic are to foster the user's creativity and help build effective song composition and audio production skills. This is achieved with the aid of step-by-step examples, providing opportunities to compose, record and mix entire productions into a satisfying whole.

The powerful production features of Logic are discovered along the way including:

MIDI and audio recording
Audio Objects and Effects
Using the Track Mixer
Track Automation
Audio Window
Sample Edit Window
Event List
Hyper Edit - including Drum Editor
Matrix Editor
Score Editor
Transform window

PC Publishing

Export House, 130 Vale Road, Tonbridge, Kent TN9 1SP, UK
Tel 01732 770893 • Fax 01732 770268 • e-mail info@pc-publishing.com
Website http://www.pc-publishing.com

Check our website!
www.pc-publishing.com

Get Creative
with
Cubase VST

Keith Gemmell

208 pp • 244 x 172 mm • illustrated
ISBN 1870775 75 9 • £14.95

- For PC and Mac
- With CD of Cubase and audio files
- Compose, arrange, record and mix your music
- Learn by doing with practical projects
- Record and edit with MIDI
- Use General MIDI, VST instruments and plug-ins
- Record, treat and manipulate audio

Do you want to learn the basics of composition and arranging, and find out how to sequence, record and mix your compositions using Cubase VST? If so, this book is for you.

Get Creative with Cubase VST will help you understand the composition process. You'll learn how to get the ideas in the first place, and how to develop, record and mix them into a satisfying whole.

Practical projects are the essence of this book - working through them and comparing your results with the examples on the CD will provide a clear insight into the creative process. And you'll be learning how to use Cubase VST at the same time.

Get Creative with Cubase VST shows you how to:

- Conceive musical ideas and develop them
- Understand melody, harmony and rhythm, the building blocks of composition
- Use MIDI to emulate real instruments like woodwinds, brass, strings and guitars
- Record vocals and real instruments using Cubase audio tracks
- Use Score edit to produce professional music parts

Read this book and discover the art of writing and producing music as you master the functions of Cubase VST 5 itself. By using it. Creatively of course!

Keith Gemmell is a composer, arranger and a lecturer in Popular Music and Music Technology at Mid Kent College in the UK.

PC Publishing

Export House, 130 Vale Road, Tonbridge, Kent TN9 1SP, UK
Tel 01732 770893 • Fax 01732 770268 • e-mail info@pc-publishing.com
Website http://www.pc-publishing.com

Check our website!
www.pc-publishing.com